The Writer's Digest
GUIDE TO MANUSCRIPT FORMATS

The Writer's Digest
GUIDE TO MANUSCRIPT FORMATS

Dian Dincin Buchman & Seli Groves

Writer's Digest Books

Cincinnati, Ohio

The Writer's Digest Guide to Manuscript Formats.
Copyright © 1987 by Dian Dincin Buchman and Seli Groves.
Printed and bound in the United States of America. All rights
reserved. No part of this book may be reproduced in any form
or by any electronic or mechanical means including
information storage and retrieval systems without permission
in writing from the publisher, except by a reviewer, who may
quote brief passages in a review. Published by Writer's Digest
Books, an imprint of F&W Publications, Inc., 1507 Dana
Avenue, Cincinnati, Ohio 45207. First edition.

92 91 90 89 88   5 4 3 2

Library of Congress Cataloging-in-Publication Data

Buchman, Dian Dincin.
  The Writer's Digest guide to manuscript formats.

  Includes index.
  1. Manuscript preparation (Authorship)—Handbooks,
manuals, etc. I. Groves, Seli. II. Title.
PN160.B78 1987   808'.02   87-31815
ISBN 0-89879-293-2

Design by Carol Buchanan.

To our colleagues of the Council of Writers Organizations whose vision for all writers is one we share.

ACKNOWLEDGMENTS

Our thanks to Freddy Groves and Caitlin Buchman—who think they know all they did for us, but who really did so much more—and to Kirk Polking and Carol Cartaino who got this book started, and to Jean Fredette and Dawn Korth who saw it through to the "light at the end of the tunnel," and to Howard Wells and the production staff at Writer's Digest Books.

We also want to thank our friends and colleagues for their help in the preparation of this book, among them: The American Medical Writers Association; Sylvia Bashline, Executive Director, the Outdoor Writers Association of America; Michelle Bekey and Richard Sherer of the Independent Writers of Southern California; William J. Bell, creator and head writer of *The Bold and the Beautiful* and *The Young and the Restless;* Alexandra Cantor and Mary Lou Theopholis-Saltonstall of the American Society of Journalists and Authors; Capital Cities/ABC (with special thanks to David Dyer, Audrey Fecht, Vic Ghidalia, Fran Gianni, Maxine Levinson and Anne Marie Ricitelli); Mary Carlin, New Dramatists; Michael Catalano Public Relations, CBS (with special thanks to Janet Storm and Ed Devlin); Isolde Chapin, Executive Director, Washington Independent Writers; Mary Higgins Clark, President, Mystery Writers of America; Columbia Pictures Television (with special thanks to Carla Princi); Anita Diamant, literary agent and President, Overseas Press Club; Joanne Douglas Public Relations; Charlie Earle Public Relations; Diane Eckert and Richard Wilson of King Features; Tania Grossinger Public Relations, Linda C. Groth, Mildred Hird, foreign rights agent; Paul Kadetz. Dramatists Guild; James Kepler of the Independent Writers of Chicago; Doe Lang, President, *Charismedia;* Lincoln Center Library of the Performing Arts, New York; The Lippin Group; Douglas Marland, head writer, *As the World Turns;* Donald McKay, Esq., pro bono adviser to the Council of Writers Organizations; Robert Scott Milne, Travel Writers Market Newsletter; Barbara Mogulescu, National Association of Science Writers (with special thanks to Diane McGurgan, Executive Director, and Diana Benzaia); NBC (with special thanks to Dorothy Austin, Charlie Barrett, Lee Fryd, Rolf Gompertz, Rosemary Keenan, Rob Maynor, and Matt Messina); Esther Nelson of Dimension 5; Nena O'Neill; Alice Harron Orr, and Herma Werner of the Romance Writers of America; Ronnie Paris, playwright; Holly Redell, Executive Director, Council of Writers Organizations; Steve Reichl Associates, Ann Reit, Executive Editor, Scholastic Books; Trumbull Rogers and Elizabeth Burpee, co-directors, Editorial Freelancers Association; Susan Savage, Esq. of Saatchi and Saatchi Compton for Procter and Gamble Productions; Ron Scott Public Relations, Barbara Seaman; Soap Opera Digest (with special thanks to Meredith Brown and Lynn Davey); Elyse Sommer; Eddy Steinberg of ArtChips; Jerome S. Traum, Esq., Claire Walter of the United States Ski Writers Association; Jim Warren Public Relations; Writers Guild of America, East (with special thanks to Mona Mangan and James Kaye).

September, 1987
New York

Seli Groves and
Dian Dincin Buchman

INTRODUCTION

We, the authors of this book, have worked in the media for many years. During our long writing and editing experience (including books, articles, scripts and columns), we have learned (sometimes the hard way) that the presentation of a professional-looking manuscript or letter to an editor or an agent is the first important step toward publication. We've also worked with other writers and editors and frequently noted their complete confusion or frustration in regard to manuscript format and submission. Indeed editors say many writers haven't the least idea where to begin in preparing their written submissions.

Writers need a guide, we said. And that's how *The Writer's Digest Guide to Manuscript Formats* came to be.

At first we planned to write a relatively simple visual aids resource book to assist writers with their format problems. But as we worked we became more and more aware of the need to include information on the presentation and submission of all kinds of written material in this sometimes tedious and complex process. So our small book evolved into a complete guide.

And a guide is just what this book is. Throughout we've been quite specific with formatting details—how many spaces down, how wide the margins, where to slug or paginate, etc. Our diagrams, At-a-Glance guides, letters and sample manuscript pages are the results of extensive research and interviews with experts (agents, editors, publishers, producers) to find out what they hope and expect to see in the submissions they receive: good, clean, professional-looking copy that is easy to read. Please understand, however, that *our directions are not graven in stone.* An editor or publisher will not reject your script or short story simply because you didn't tab in the suggested number of spaces or drop a certain number of lines. But, in general, if your work is properly presented, it will have a greater chance for acceptance or publication.

Of course, it's the content and style in your work that ultimately count in determining a final sale. But editors and publishers are human and subject to normal first impressions; they will initially judge your work by its "look." If you send in a smudged, no margin, coffee-stained, dot-matrix, difficult-to-read manuscript that signals "AMATEUR," your Good Impression Index plummets to zero.

Dressing for success in the business world means putting on the clothes that make an important statement, which says you know this is where you belong, and, by inference, that you know your stuff. It's analogous to the writer presenting his or her work in the generally accepted format that tells editors and publishers that you appear to know your subject or writing area well.

Knowing format is important for all writers. For new writers, it's essential. Since you can't sell your novel or article on a very long track record, or any track record at all, at least presenting your work in a professional manner gives you that extra edge, a selling point in your favor. As writers, we would long ago have appreciated a book like this ourselves. (Remember, you're getting the benefit between two covers of what we had to search out from innumerable sources.)

As editors, in the past we would have liked to show our writers how to present a manuscript to us. Now, when we do editorial work in the future, we know just the book to suggest to our contributors.

Now that our research is finished, we appreciate even more that manuscript preparation and submission often present awesome problems, especially to beginning writers. We understand that lack of direction and the inevitable wheelspinning are an anti-climax to the writing process itself. With this guide, we hope you will be able to short-cut those formatting problems and save time and energy for more writing projects. And most important, we hope you will be able to present the professional package that best reflects the quality of your writing—to make your editors say, "Yes, this writer *cares* about his/her work. We'd like to publish this."

Seli Groves   dian Lincin buchman

AT-A-GLANCE GUIDE TO TYPING

Paper   Use only good quality 20-pound bond. *Never* use erasable paper. Editors cannot make corrections on it because it smudges. Computer paper should be laser cut (clean-cut) so that separated pages have sharp, clean edges.

Use only one side of the page.

Type Size   10 pitch pica is preferred. Elite is acceptable.

Ribbons   Use clean, clear, black ribbons.

Corrections   Queries, proposals, and cover letters should not show penciled corrections. Correction tape and/or liquid correction fluid can be used if invisible in a photocopy. In your drafts and *final* copy, feel free to use tape, liquid correction fluid, and/or proof mark corrections (see pages 163-65).

Headers (Slugs), Footers

The copy you see at the top of a page that is not part of the manuscript per se is the *header* (or *slug*); the copy at the bottom is the *footer*. The material acts as a running identification mechanism. It tells you the name of the book or chapter and the page number. If labeling is done correctly, the editor always knows where he or she is in the manuscript. Computer users may find that their word-processor programs have functions that allow them to set up running heads and running feet automatically, along with page numbers and text. See sample header, page 6.

Margins   Allow 1-1½ or more inches around text. Wide margins enhance appearance and provide sufficient space for editing notes or comments.

Typing   You can set your typewriter's margins so that you can type within certain space limits. To retain control over the hidden bottom margin, put a light pencil mark on the paper some two to four lines before the end of the last paragraph. If you use a blue nonreproducing pencil, the marks are not picked up by a photocopier when copies are made. If you intend to use that particular page as an original, however, be sure to erase any penciled-in notations.

Computer   Computer word processor programs instruct the printer on how to set up margins on a page. Most have small margins. Refer to your manual to reset these margins.

All manuscript pages   As a general rule, for top margin, drop 4 lines and start at left margin. Type in a *slug* or *header*—a shorthand book title—plus your name in left-hand corner of page. Type a page number in the right-hand corner. If using a computer, check directions that combine header (slug) and page numbering.

For second and subsequent pages of each chapter, drop 6 lines from header/slug and number and start text.

NUMBERING AND SPACING IN A TYPED MANUSCRIPT

It's easier to number than you thought. Number your manuscript pages sequentially—1, 2, 3, and up.

The exceptions are front matter and illustrative matter such as charts, maps, diagrams, tables, photos, illustrations. Let us explain: Front matter is typed after your manuscript is finished. Technically, it is not part of your manuscript. Also, since each item is presented on a separate page, there is no need to worry about where it goes; the editor will arrange its placement.

It's a little more complicated to present tables, charts, maps, and illustrations, since you will not include them within the text but will make reference to each insertion (see At-a-Glance Guide to Numbering and Spacing). Also each *group* (more than one) of such illustrations has its own number sequence. For example: tables can be numbered as Table 1, Table 2, etc., as can groups of charts, maps, diagrams. Figures (illustrations)—see section on book illustrations, page 171—are numbered as Fig. 1, Fig. 2, Fig. 3, etc. Read this section for full instructions for developing your illustration codes and subgrouping codes.

AT-A-GLANCE GUIDE TO NUMBERING AND SPACING

Preferred Placement of Numbers	Right-hand corner. Typewriter: 3/4" (4-5 spaces) down from top right-hand margin. Computer: place on right-hand margin on same line as head (slug).
Tip	A preferred placement is just that—you can also center numbers at the top or bottom.
Typewriter	Number text sequentially in Arabic numerals, i.e., 1, 2, 3, 4, 5.
Computer	Most word-processing programs number text automatically; however, many place the numbers at the bottom of the page. If you choose to use the preferred placement of numbers, check your manual for instructions on page numbering. Header (slug) is run on left, number on right. (See sample.)
Tip	If your computer places page numbers automatically on the bottom of the page, and you can't change the instructions but choose to follow the preferred upper-right hand corner placement of numbers, allow for a slightly deeper top margin and later type or handwrite the numbers on the final draft. Erase the old number with liquid correction fluid.
Numbering First Drafts: Long Manuscript	It is often necessary to work out sections and chapters of book manuscripts in a nonsequential way. When constructing a manuscript in parts, number each part separately. This allows you to delete, add, and reconstruct as you go along.
Final draft	Combine the revised sections for typing of final manuscript. Number in sequence. If your final manuscript is finished but unpaginated, lightly handwrite the numbers with nonreproducing blue pencil and type in later.

Do Not Number the Following Kinds of Pages

Title page	Place on separate page. Do not number (see pages 7, 31).
Charts, diagrams, maps, illustrations	Do not type into text. Instead *indicate* in text where the table, chart, etc. will be. Usual placement is after the paragraph that first mentions the table, etc. (also see pages 172-73—Illustrations). Double-space before and after your indicator.
Indicator sample	**[Chart 2B MAGNESIUM about here]**
Tables	Margins: Type 1½" from top of page. Space: Double-space between lines of table Allow 3 spaces between columns Line up: by decimals Dollar Signs: Type $ at top of column. Percentage Signs: Type % at top of column.

Lines on a Page

	As a general rule, try to type about the same number of lines on each page.
Exceptions	Avoid typing a heading or the first lines of a new paragraph at the bottom of a page. Instead, start a new page. Don't begin a page with the last line of a paragraph. Instead, shorten the preceding page and carry over at least two lines to the top of the new page.

Spacing of Book Manuscript Text

Paragraph indention	Indent first line of paragraph 5 spaces on typewriter. Six-space tab on word processor is also acceptable.
Double-space	The general rule is to double-space all text pages. In addition, double-space proposals, queries, personal bio, Introduction, chapter outlines, Preface, Dedication, Epigraph, Table of Contents (see exceptions), Notes, List of Tables, List of Illustrations, captions, Appendix (see exceptions), Bibliography (see exceptions), References, Glossary, Index. Double-space after chapter headings, and between chapter headings and first subheading entry.
Exceptions	Publisher's request to triple- or single-space Some business reports Certain business proposals Dissertations

Single-space	Use single spacing (no empty lines between text), but double-space *between* each item, in: Quotations Bibliographies Notes (some) tables—refer to publisher's guidelines
Triple-space	Triple-space (2 empty lines) before and after a blocked, indented quotation that interrupts text.
Quadruple-space	Quadruple-space (3 empty lines—start text on 4th line) between title and text of: Biography Notes Reference Notes Acknowledgments Bibliography Appendix
Chapter headings	Skip 3 spaces after chapter number or period following chapter number.
Long headings	Single-space two-line headings. Divide by looks and sense. No line should be too long or too short. Don't divide words in centered headings.
Space after heading	Don't place a heading at the bottom of a page. Always have at least 2 lines of text after a heading. Leave at least 2 spaces above and 2 below flush left and centered headings.
Spaces between words	Skip one space after all words, commas, semicolons, colons, question marks, and exclamation points within a sentence. Skip two spaces after punctuation ending a sentence.
Spacing within text	Do *not* press the space bar for space between letters of words; or before, after, or between hyphens or dashes.
First page of every major division of a book Each chapter Table of Contents Preface Introduction List of Tables List of Illustrations Bibliography Appendix	Begin on new page. Count 16-18 spaces down from top of page. Center each heading. Capitalize each heading. Don't type a page number.

HEADER (SLUG) SAMPLE

Drop 1-1½" (6-8 lines)

Left margin

Page number at right margin—(same line as slug)

Drop 6-8 lines

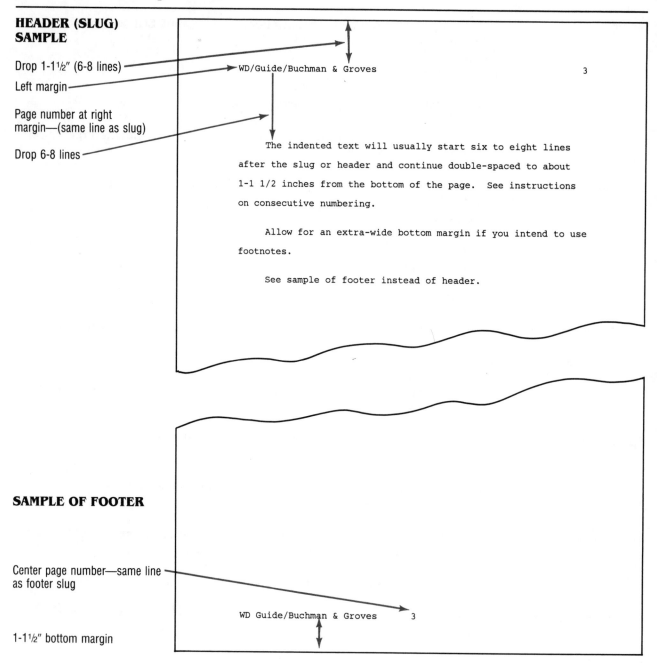

WD/Guide/Buchman & Groves   3

       The indented text will usually start six to eight lines after the slug or header and continue double-spaced to about 1-1 1/2 inches from the bottom of the page. See instructions on consecutive numbering.

       Allow for an extra-wide bottom margin if you intend to use footnotes.

       See sample of footer instead of header.

SAMPLE OF FOOTER

Center page number—same line as footer slug

1-1½" bottom margin

WD Guide/Buchman & Groves   3

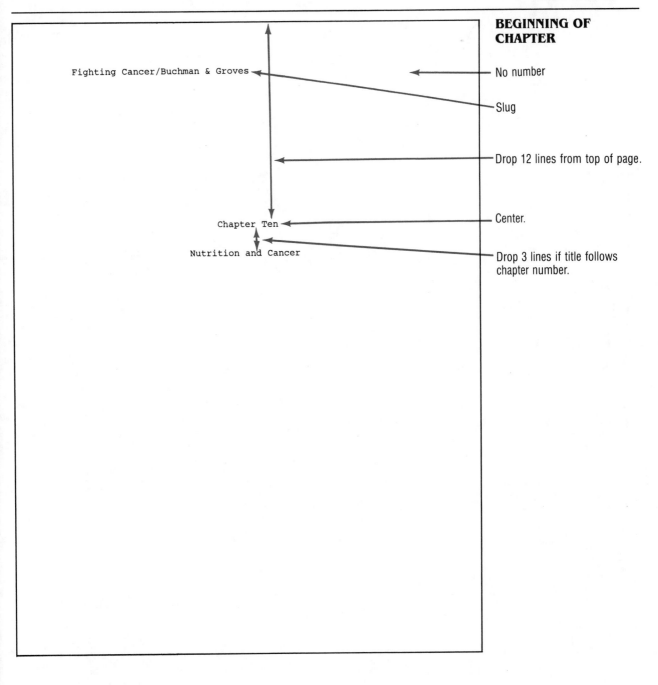

BEGINNING OF
CHAPTER

Fighting Cancer/Buchman & Groves

No number

Slug

Drop 12 lines from top of page.

Chapter Ten

Center.

Nutrition and Cancer

Drop 3 lines if title follows
chapter number.

Books

NONFICTION

PROPOSALS/QUERIES

Many writers have become *proposal phobics* (or *query-phobics*) and would rather write a full book than attempt one of those (unnecessarily) dreaded necessities of publishing life. After all, it's not easy to come up with a sure-sale way to distill the essence of what will be a work of several hundred pages into a few pages, or a few paragraphs, or even a few lines. (The last phrase refers to the editorial credo that every work could be—but in practice almost never is—sold on the basis of no more than three sentences, and everything else in the proposal is merely "commentary.")

There's no magic formula for devising a proposal that produces contracts and generous advances. The sale of your work depends on the same basic, prosaic elements that apply in the commercial world: Is there genuine interest in your idea? How good is your idea? How well can you package it? In other words: Can your proposal sell your book?

This section will answer those questions—and other questions almost every writer has wondered about at some time or another.

Along with discussions about proposals for both nonfiction and fiction books, we have provided sample proposals for both types of books, plus sample query and cover letters. Using these samples as models for your own work will assure that you will never suffer an attack of acute *proposal- or query-phobia.*

The Question Many Writers Are Too Embarrassed to Ask

Many writers go through life never daring to ask the question they believe has already been answered for every other writer they know. It's as if by asking *What's the difference between a proposal and an outline?*, they risk exposing themselves as perpetual innocents when, by the time they're ready to submit a book proposal, they should be seasoned veterans.

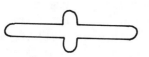

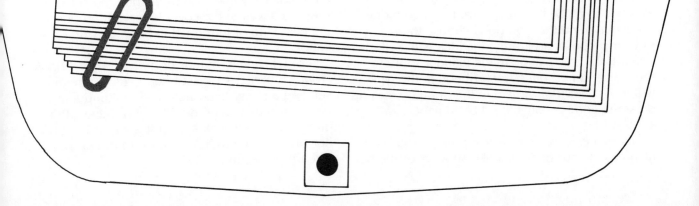

The fact is, most people don't really know the answer. Some believe an outline is submitted only for fiction books, while others insist it's used only for nonfiction. Some writers think the concepts are synonymous. Well, sometimes they are. But there is a fine line of difference between the two forms, and knowing that difference is like finally mastering the subjunctive tense: maybe a lot of other people will never notice that you know what it is and how to use it, but you'll always have that sense of satisfaction that comes with having special knowledge.

The following is a simple explanation of the difference between these two important forms:

The Anatomy Lesson

Think of your *book* as a completed body of work. Imagine that the *proposal*—which can be made up of all or some of the following elements: query letter, proposal, outline, cover letter, "bio," etc.—constitutes the body's muscles and sinew structures.

The *outline* could be called the "bare bones" or skeletal structure on which everything ultimately hangs.

Some Specifics

The *proposal* sets forth the basic premise of an idea for a written work in a *package* designed, essentially, to sell the book. A proposal can be long or short; a detailed description or a simplified overview. It can discuss, at length, the contents of the book and the planned preparation, including the book's format (sections, chapters, bibliographies, glossaries, chapter synopses, etc.). Or it can present the essence of the idea in a briefer form. Whatever form your proposal takes, remember to present your ideas with the flair and the style to make the reader want to read more.

Keep in mind that you don't choose the length of your proposal arbitrarily: the idea is to sell the book. If the sale can be made using a shorter form, fine; if not, put a fresh ribbon in the typewriter or a new Daisywheel in the printer, stock up on some good twenty-pound bond paper, and start writing.

An *outline*, if well-constructed, helps you cover all areas of your book. It's like an X-ray of the ba-sic structures of the book. It can be a chapter-by-chapter detailed description of the book's contents, or especially in fiction, of its plots, subplots, action, and character interaction.

Besides being used as part of a proposal, an outline can be helpful in the actual writing process.

To extend the skeletal metaphor even further, a good outline is like the framework of a building: every I-bar and T-bar is meant to hold a certain structure. However, just as an architect can have changes made in the structural framework if needed, so, too, can you make changes in your outline. It should be a flexible guide, not a constraint on your work. For example, in fiction, the characters often dictate the way situations will develop, and the writer then has to make adjustments accordingly. In nonfiction, research may produce a fact that may alter the outlined approach you set up. Although a good outline takes quite a bit of time and effort, in the long run, it saves unnecessary work.

To Query or Not to Query?

This is another question writers ask. There have been several schools of thought on the subject: Some writers choose to query an editor with the idea before submitting a formal proposal, especially if they're unsure about the types of manuscripts the publisher handles. Others think a query is just an extension of good manners, i.e., asking for an invitation to submit your material instead of sending it along cold. Pro-query people also point out that these letters act as introductions between an editor and an unknown writer.

Still others see a query letter as an unnecessary step, pointing out that a well-constructed cover letter that accompanies the proposal is all that's required. They maintain that a good idea that's presented well in the cover letter and proposal is the best kind of introduction between writer and editor.

Michael Larsen, author of *How to Write a Book Proposal* (Writer's Digest Books), recommends sending a query letter before submitting a proposal. And there's no doubt that a well-written query could very well key up the interest of an editor who may be more receptive to the proposal when it comes in.

MORE QUESTIONS WRITERS WANT TO ASK

Are Proposals Really Necessary?

Some people say they never send in anything more than a bare outline and still make a sale. But they're a tiny minority in the ranks of successful writers. While it's true that some books were sold on the basis of an idea or a title, most sales are made with well-presented proposals.

How Long Should a Proposal Be?

As we noted earlier, if you can sum up the entire idea of your work in no more than three sentences, you have a complete proposal. But the fact is most of us need to do more to persuade an editor to consider the work. The answer to the "how long should it be" question really is: *as long as it needs to be.* Some may run for fifty or more pages. Others can say it all in a few paragraphs.

Remember that a proposal in publishing is a lot like a marriage proposal. Both set forth offers *made in anticipation of acceptance.* Both also need to make offers in ways that put the hopeful suitors in the best possible light.

PROPOSAL FORMATS

Nonfiction

The following section will deal with the various forms that comprise a generally accepted proposal package for nonfiction work.

Among the elements that will be discussed in this section are the following:

The Query Letter

The Proposal

The Cover Letter—There are two types of cover letters: one accompanies your unsolicited manuscript (it's more like a query); the other accompanies a proposal that has been requested in reply to the self-contained query letter.

We'll also give you instructive samples of each of the documents that we discuss.

We have created a hypothetical nonfiction work, *Skateboarding in America.* All of the discussions and samples that are presented in this section will deal with this hypothetical book.

The Starting Point: Query Letters

As we discussed earlier, some writers don't send query letters. But the authors feel that when there's any question of whether to do so or not, it's better to err on the side of commission than omission.

Specifics: Two Types of Query Letters. Before you submit a proposal, you may send a one-page, self-contained query that informs the editor that you are working on a book about skateboarding in America and that there are several reasons (which you'd cite, as in the example further on) why you believe he or she would want to see your detailed proposal on this subject.

Note: If you are sending multiple or simultaneous query letters (sending them to many publishing houses at the same time) let everyone who gets a copy know you're doing this.

And when we say *copy,* we don't mean something that looks like one: we mean a document that looks like an original. If you work with a computer and your program supports a mail-merge feature, it's relatively easy to produce several "originals." Or you can produce one original and after you've printed it out, you simply edit it on disk, deleting one address and salutation and inserting the next one. If you use the latter method, be sure to print out with a carbon, or use two-part computer paper, which produces a simultaneous hard copy. This will give you a record of names and addresses to whom you sent your query; or you can photocopy each submission for your records.

If you use a typewriter, type up one original, leaving room for the inclusion of separate names, addresses, and salutations. Make photocopies of the original and reinsert each new copy in the typewriter; type in the specific names and addresses.

Be Prepared

It's a good idea to have the proposal completed and ready to go when you send out your queries. This means you should also have at least two to three chapters of your nonfiction book ready for submission with the proposal. (Fiction writers, especially new writers, often have to submit an entire manuscript with the proposal.)

NONFICTION QUERY LETTER SAMPLE #1
This is sent out before proposal is submitted

Letter is in block form, single-spaced

Letterhead

Drop 4-6 lines.

Drop 4 lines.
Addressee

Salutation

Book premise

Cite reasons book should be written, including current interest and potential.

What does book offer? and to whom?

Cite readiness to send material.

Why you are the right person to write this book

Note multiple queries if relevant.

Simple closing

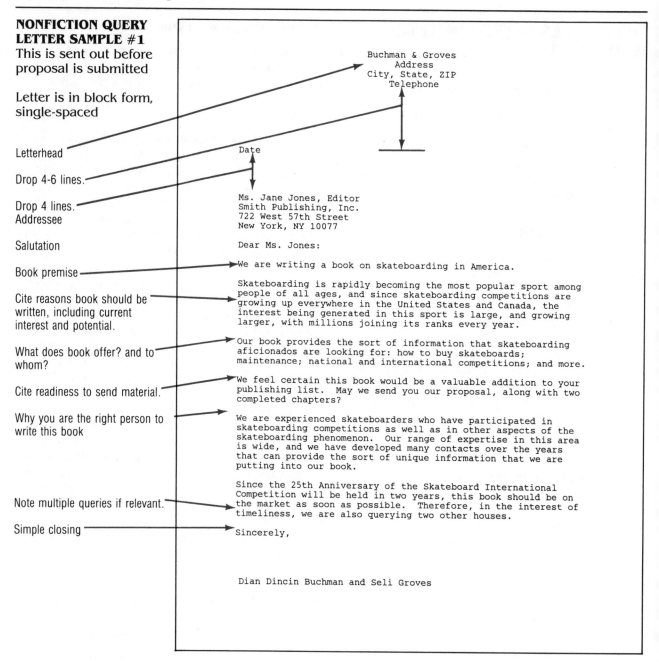

Buchman & Groves
Address
City, State, ZIP
Telephone

Date

Ms. Jane Jones, Editor
Smith Publishing, Inc.
722 West 57th Street
New York, NY 10077

Dear Ms. Jones:

We are writing a book on skateboarding in America.

Skateboarding is rapidly becoming the most popular sport among people of all ages, and since skateboarding competitions are growing up everywhere in the United States and Canada, the interest being generated in this sport is large, and growing larger, with millions joining its ranks every year.

Our book provides the sort of information that skateboarding aficionados are looking for: how to buy skateboards; maintenance; national and international competitions; and more.

We feel certain this book would be a valuable addition to your publishing list. May we send you our proposal, along with two completed chapters?

We are experienced skateboarders who have participated in skateboarding competitions as well as in other aspects of the skateboarding phenomenon. Our range of expertise in this area is wide, and we have developed many contacts over the years that can provide the sort of unique information that we are putting into our book.

Since the 25th Anniversary of the Skateboard International Competition will be held in two years, this book should be on the market as soon as possible. Therefore, in the interest of timeliness, we are also querying two other houses.

Sincerely,

Dian Dincin Buchman and Seli Groves

Remember, the prime directive of a query letter is to initiate interest in your book and to solicit a request by the editor to see the proposal, including two or three chapters—or, perhaps, the entire manuscript.

Therefore, keep in mind that regardless of which type of query letter you send, it needs to have much the same content as a proposal would, to wit:

What the subject is
Why a book on this subject would sell well
Who the readership is

Why you are the right person to write this book
How soon you can have the book ready for submission

You can compare the query letter samples that appear on these two pages.

If your original query—the self-contained version sent before submitting your proposal—elicited an editor's request to review the proposal and chapters, you would submit them with a cover letter.

The sample on page 14 provides a general guide to preparing a cover letter.

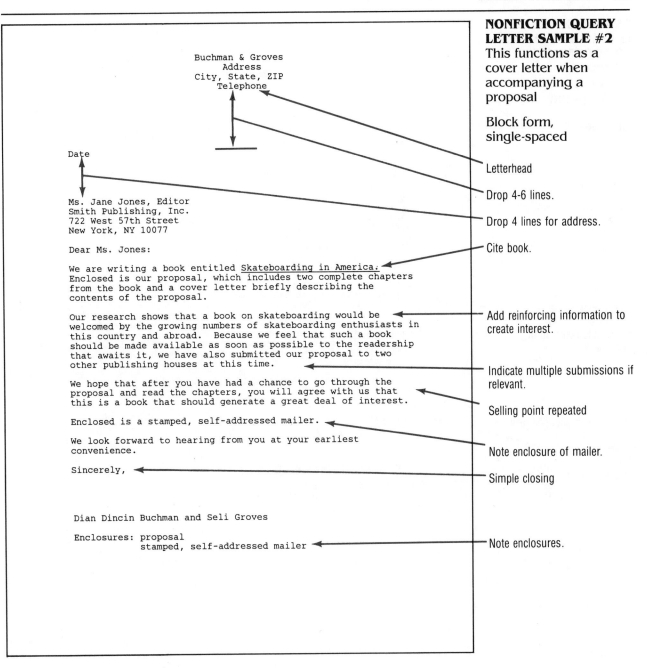

NONFICTION QUERY LETTER SAMPLE #2
This functions as a cover letter when accompanying a proposal

Block form, single-spaced

Letterhead

Drop 4-6 lines.

Drop 4 lines for address.

Cite book.

Add reinforcing information to create interest.

Indicate multiple submissions if relevant.

Selling point repeated

Note enclosure of mailer.

Simple closing

Note enclosures.

**SAMPLE COVER
LETTER (REPLY)
TO ACCOMPANY
PROPOSAL**
Block form,
single-spaced

Letterhead

Drop 6 lines.

Drop 4 lines for name and
address.

Cite reply to your query.

Repeat book name.

Briefly note contents of
proposal.

Cite enclosed stamped mailer.

Simple closing

Note enclosures.

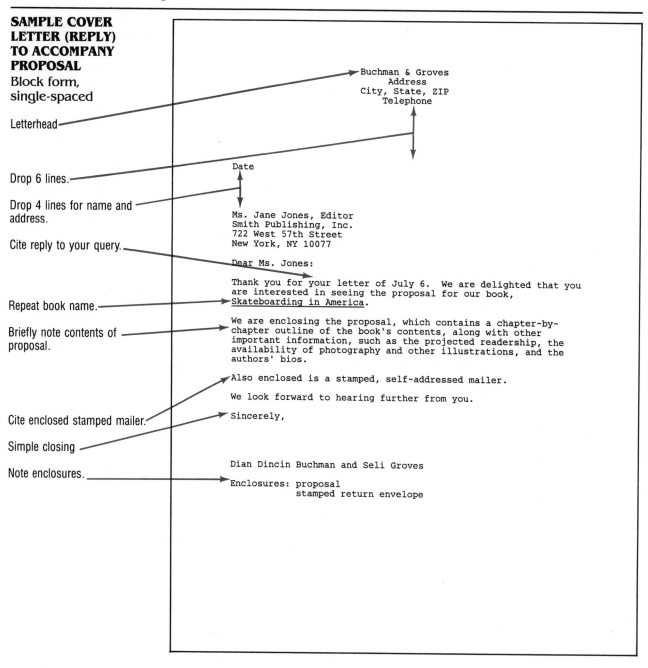

```
                                        Buchman & Groves
                                            Address
                                        City, State, ZIP
                                          Telephone



                        Date


                        Ms. Jane Jones, Editor
                        Smith Publishing, Inc.
                        722 West 57th Street
                        New York, NY 10077

                        Dear Ms. Jones:

                        Thank you for your letter of July 6.  We are delighted that you
                        are interested in seeing the proposal for our book,
                        Skateboarding in America.

                        We are enclosing the proposal, which contains a chapter-by-
                        chapter outline of the book's contents, along with other
                        important information, such as the projected readership, the
                        availability of photography and other illustrations, and the
                        authors' bios.

                        Also enclosed is a stamped, self-addressed mailer.

                        We look forward to hearing further from you.

                        Sincerely,


                        Dian Dincin Buchman and Seli Groves

                        Enclosures: proposal
                                    stamped return envelope
```

To Whom Are You Speaking?

When you write a proposal, keep in mind that you are addressing two audiences:
You are writing this TO the editor; and
You are writing this FOR your readers.

That's not as difficult as it sounds. The editor needs information that will persuade him or her to, in turn, try to persuade the publisher to sign the author and publish the book. That type of information includes all factors that deal with its salability, such as its readership, its importance in the marketplace, etc. (You'll see more about this farther on.)

However, another equally important selling point is your writing style. So, while you compile an informative proposal for the editor, be sure you make it as bright, crisp, interesting, and brilliant as we know you're going to write the book itself.

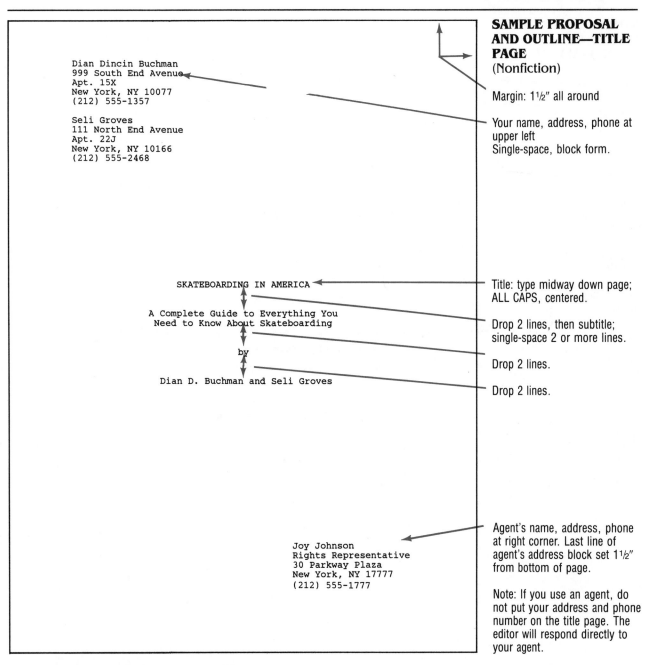

SAMPLE PROPOSAL AND OUTLINE—TITLE PAGE
(Nonfiction)

Margin: 1½″ all around

Your name, address, phone at upper left
Single-space, block form.

Title: type midway down page; ALL CAPS, centered.

Drop 2 lines, then subtitle; single-space 2 or more lines.

Drop 2 lines.

Drop 2 lines.

Agent's name, address, phone at right corner. Last line of agent's address block set 1½″ from bottom of page.

Note: If you use an agent, do not put your address and phone number on the title page. The editor will respond directly to your agent.

Within the diagram:

Dian Dincin Buchman
999 South End Avenue
Apt. 15X
New York, NY 10077
(212) 555-1357

Seli Groves
111 North End Avenue
Apt. 22J
New York, NY 10166
(212) 555-2468

SKATEBOARDING IN AMERICA

A Complete Guide to Everything You
Need to Know About Skateboarding

by

Dian D. Buchman and Seli Groves

Joy Johnson
Rights Representative
30 Parkway Plaza
New York, NY 17777
(212) 555-1777

THE PROPOSAL—AT LAST!

On the following pages, you'll see a sample proposal for a hypothetical non-fiction book by the authors, called *Skateboarding in America*.

The elements included in this sample are the following:

1. Title page (diagrammed to indicate spacing and margins)
2. Table of contents
3. Introduction—which includes:

a) Overview—includes information about the book, the readership, the competition (if any), number of pages, illustrations, etc.
b) Resources needed to complete this book (expenses necessary for research)
c) Authors' bios

4. The outline—chapter-by-chapter breakdown of the book's content
5. Sample chapters

**SAMPLE TABLE OF
CONTENTS
(PROPOSAL)**

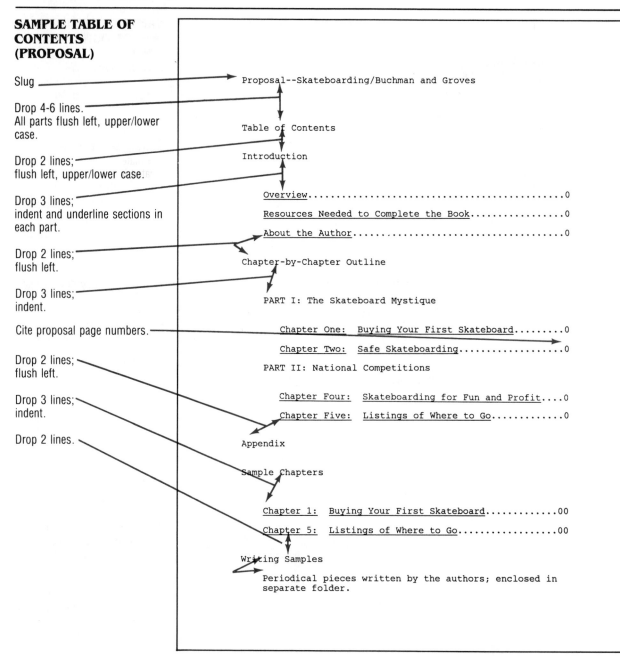

Slug

Drop 4-6 lines.
All parts flush left, upper/lower
case.

Drop 2 lines;
flush left, upper/lower case.

Drop 3 lines;
indent and underline sections in
each part.

Drop 2 lines;
flush left.

Drop 3 lines;
indent.

Cite proposal page numbers.

Drop 2 lines;
flush left.

Drop 3 lines;
indent.

Drop 2 lines.

Proposal--Skateboarding/Buchman and Groves

Table of Contents

Introduction

Overview..0
Resources Needed to Complete the Book................0
About the Author.....................................0

Chapter-by-Chapter Outline

PART I: The Skateboard Mystique

Chapter One: Buying Your First Skateboard.........0
Chapter Two: Safe Skateboarding...................0

PART II: National Competitions

Chapter Four: Skateboarding for Fun and Profit....0
Chapter Five: Listings of Where to Go.............0

Appendix

Sample Chapters

Chapter 1: Buying Your First Skateboard.............00
Chapter 5: Listings of Where to Go..................00

Writing Samples

Periodical pieces written by the authors; enclosed in
separate folder.

Some proposals for nonfiction books contain
an appendix, part of the book's back matter,
which includes peripheral information. In the appendix of this book, "Et Cetera," you'll find easy-
to-use checklists to help you through each step in
the preparation of a proposal.

Proposal--Skateboarding/Buchman and Groves

Supporting Documents

Articles from Business Week, Forbes, and the Los Angeles Times
indicating the growing importance of skateboarding to industry;
enclosed in a separate folder.

Athletics for Fun, by Desmond Dumont (Healthy Hearts Press,
London, England); enclosed. See Chapter 10, Skateboards for
Health.

SAMPLE TABLE OF CONTENTS (PROPOSAL)—SECOND PAGE

Do not number

Drop 2 lines;
cite material and indicate where located in proposal.

SAMPLE PROPOSAL PAGE

Slug: top of page

Show page number on right.

Start 3-4″ (18-24 lines) down.

Double-space.

Underline.

Drop 4 lines; indent each paragraph. Open with a "grabber."

Repeat title and subtitle.

Who will buy it and why; what is its potential?

Length of book

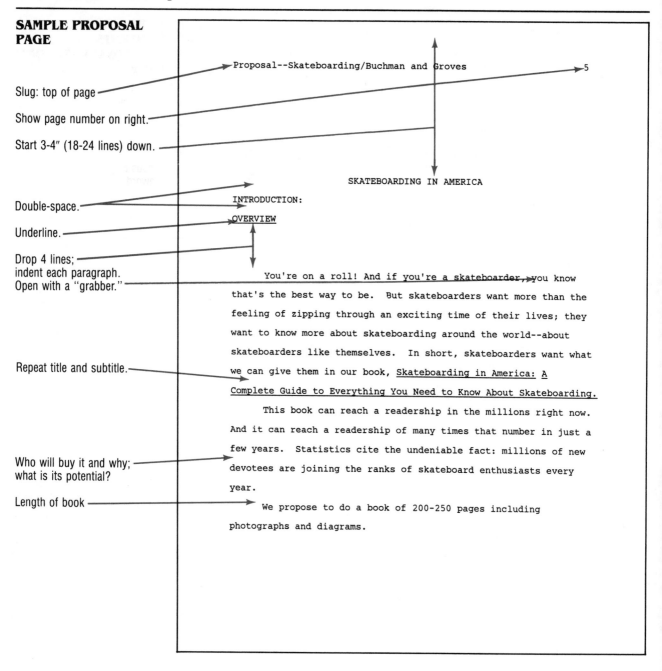

Proposal--Skateboarding/Buchman and Groves   5

SKATEBOARDING IN AMERICA

INTRODUCTION:

OVERVIEW

        You're on a roll! And if you're a skateboarder, you know
that's the best way to be. But skateboarders want more than the
feeling of zipping through an exciting time of their lives; they
want to know more about skateboarding around the world--about
skateboarders like themselves. In short, skateboarders want what
we can give them in our book, Skateboarding in America: A
Complete Guide to Everything You Need to Know About Skateboarding.
        This book can reach a readership in the millions right now.
And it can reach a readership of many times that number in just a
few years. Statistics cite the undeniable fact: millions of new
devotees are joining the ranks of skateboard enthusiasts every
year.
        We propose to do a book of 200-250 pages including
photographs and diagrams.

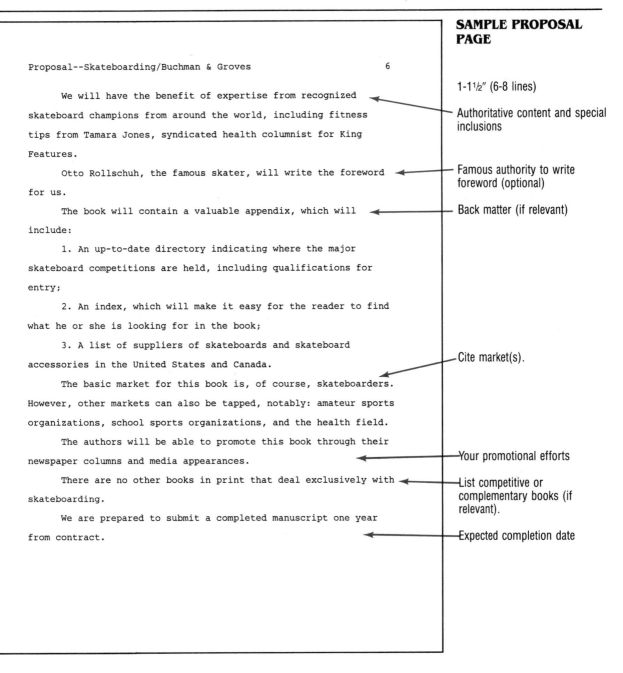

Proposal--Skateboarding/Buchman & Groves   6

We will have the benefit of expertise from recognized skateboard champions from around the world, including fitness tips from Tamara Jones, syndicated health columnist for King Features.

Otto Rollschuh, the famous skater, will write the foreword for us.

The book will contain a valuable appendix, which will include:

1. An up-to-date directory indicating where the major skateboard competitions are held, including qualifications for entry;

2. An index, which will make it easy for the reader to find what he or she is looking for in the book;

3. A list of suppliers of skateboards and skateboard accessories in the United States and Canada.

The basic market for this book is, of course, skateboarders. However, other markets can also be tapped, notably: amateur sports organizations, school sports organizations, and the health field.

The authors will be able to promote this book through their newspaper columns and media appearances.

There are no other books in print that deal exclusively with skateboarding.

We are prepared to submit a completed manuscript one year from contract.

1-1½″ (6-8 lines)

Authoritative content and special inclusions

Famous authority to write foreword (optional)

Back matter (if relevant)

Cite market(s).

Your promotional efforts

List competitive or complementary books (if relevant).

Expected completion date

SAMPLE PAGE—
Estimate of expenses to complete book

1-1½″ (6-8 lines)

Page number

Slug

Also estimate cost of drawings or other illustrations, if necessary.

Line up figures.

1-1½″ all around

```
Proposal--Skateboarding /Buchman & Groves                    8

Resources Needed to Complete This Book
     ITEM                                          PROJECTED COST
Photographs:
     The book will include photographs of
international competitions, local competitions,
school-sponsored skateboarding events, street
skateboarding.                                      $1,000.00


Permissions:
     We will be interviewing several authorites
on skateboarding, and we'll secure releases to use
these interviews or portions of them in the book.     150.00


Computer Services:
     We expect to access databases to secure the
most recent information on national and internation-
al competitions.                                      250.00


Travel:
     We will be traveling to California for a week-
long stay at the San Tomaso Skate and Surf Conven-
tion during November.                                 750.00

Typing Costs, Telephone Calls, Misc.                  200.00

TOTAL                                               $2,350.00
```

ABOUT THE AUTHOR (BIOS FOR PROPOSALS)

The next sample is a hypothetical bio (sometimes called *curriculum vitae,* and abbreviated CV) that an author would send along with a proposal.

Following are important points to remember when making up a bio:

Following are important points to remember when making up a bio:

1. It is not your life story, even though the word *bio* is short for *biography.*

2. It should include information that sells *you* as a writer on whom the editor can depend to turn out the book he or she agrees to buy.

3. If you have publishing credits, they should be cited in a certain order: name the most important credits first, followed by credits that support your expertise or background.

4. If you have no publishing credits, cite other examples of your proven dependability. (Remember: along with writing skill and style—which you will be showing in your proposal—the editor needs to know that you can follow through on a commitment.)

5. If there is more than one author, each bio is on a separate page.

6. The CV is written in third person (the preferred form). It is not recommended that it be presented in first person. *If you do use first person,* keep the *I*'s to a minimum. It's all right to have a healthy sense of self-esteem, but you can give an editor "I strain" if you sprinkle your bio with that pronoun liberally.

7. The sample shown is the third-person (preferred) version the authors are using for their hypothetical book on skateboarding.

AT-A-GLANCE GUIDE TO BIOS

The Style	Avoid being dry, academic, pretentious, or monotonous.
In first person?	NO! *Write the CV in third person* as if it is a news release about someone else. This is the *preferred* version.
Do I need to include everything I ever did?	*No, you don't!* A CV is not a resume. For example, you need a clear, concise, no-nonsense description of relevant work, hobby, and social experiences, as well as education. Mention how and why you are knowledgeable—anything to indicate your expertise and access to information.*
Should I include the titles of my publications?	Highlight the important and relevant publications. Avoid hype. If you are widely published, write up a list and add as a separate insert.
Books	Title; publisher; trade; mail order, textbook, special and subsidiary sales; one page of reviews. List by most recent in descending order.
Periodicals	Number of years you've been writing and researching and in what field or fields. List relevant articles and range of subjects; stress articles on subject of book.

*Remember, in preliminary negotiations, keep contacts and special research facts to yourself.

SAMPLE: ABOUT THE AUTHOR—Third person version (preferred style)

Slug and page number

6-8 lines from top underline title; add author's name.

Drop 4 lines.
Double-space.
Indent.
Start with anecdotal personal "grabber" linked to subject.

Cite professional expertise.

Published credits

List, or center as shown.

Cite relevant background.

Talk about book.

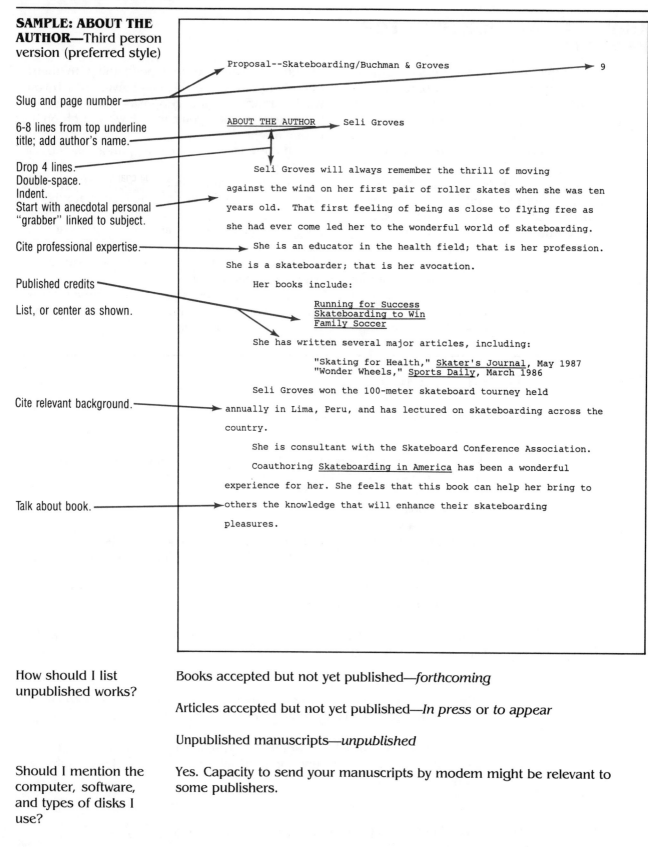

Proposal--Skateboarding/Buchman & Groves   9

ABOUT THE AUTHOR   Seli Groves

     Seli Groves will always remember the thrill of moving against the wind on her first pair of roller skates when she was ten years old. That first feeling of being as close to flying free as she had ever come led her to the wonderful world of skateboarding.

She is an educator in the health field; that is her profession. She is a skateboarder; that is her avocation.

     Her books include:

        Running for Success
        Skateboarding to Win
        Family Soccer

She has written several major articles, including:

        "Skating for Health," Skater's Journal, May 1987
        "Wonder Wheels," Sports Daily, March 1986

Seli Groves won the 100-meter skateboard tourney held annually in Lima, Peru, and has lectured on skateboarding across the country.

     She is consultant with the Skateboard Conference Association.

     Coauthoring Skateboarding in America has been a wonderful experience for her. She feels that this book can help her bring to others the knowledge that will enhance their skateboarding pleasures.

How should I list unpublished works?

Books accepted but not yet published—*forthcoming*

Articles accepted but not yet published—*In press* or *to appear*

Unpublished manuscripts—*unpublished*

Should I mention the computer, software, and types of disks I use?

Yes. Capacity to send your manuscripts by modem might be relevant to some publishers.

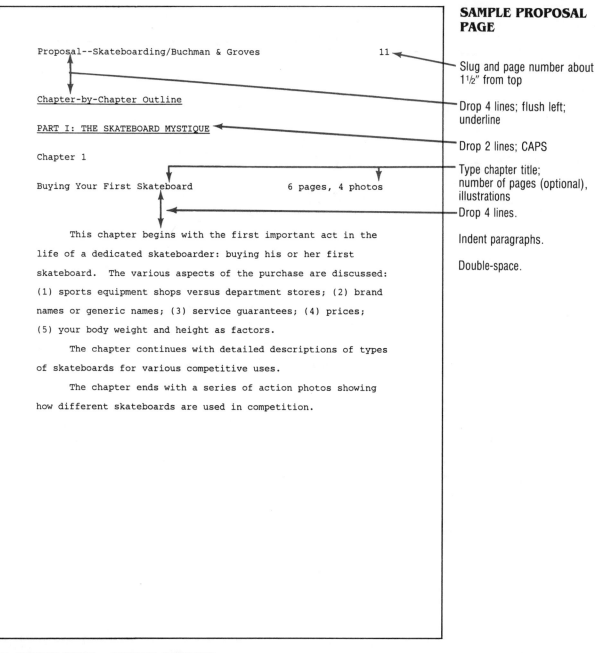

SAMPLE PROPOSAL PAGE

Proposal--Skateboarding/Buchman & Groves   11

Slug and page number about 1½" from top

Chapter-by-Chapter Outline

Drop 4 lines; flush left; underline

PART I: THE SKATEBOARD MYSTIQUE

Drop 2 lines; CAPS

Chapter 1

Buying Your First Skateboard   6 pages, 4 photos

Type chapter title; number of pages (optional), illustrations

Drop 4 lines.

    This chapter begins with the first important act in the life of a dedicated skateboarder: buying his or her first skateboard. The various aspects of the purchase are discussed: (1) sports equipment shops versus department stores; (2) brand names or generic names; (3) service guarantees; (4) prices; (5) your body weight and height as factors.

    The chapter continues with detailed descriptions of types of skateboards for various competitive uses.

    The chapter ends with a series of action photos showing how different skateboards are used in competition.

Indent paragraphs.

Double-space.

THE OUTLINE—EXPLAINED

On this and the following pages, you'll see a sample of a version of a typical chapter-by-chapter outline that is used by most writers for their proposals.

Our sample is deliberately brief. However, regardless of how short a chapter outline is, each chapter is presented on a separate page. (Okay, okay. We've all seen chapter outlines presented 1, 2, 3, etc., on one page. But we're here to give the generally accepted format. We don't mean to make you work harder; we only want you to *sell that book!*)

You'll notice certain features:

The name slug or header (your name and part of the book's title) appears on every page a few lines below the top of the page; the page number appears to the right on the same line.

The number of pages in the chapter, along with

SAMPLE PROPOSAL PAGE

Slug and page number
1½" (or 8 lines) from top

Number of pages optional

Chapter title

Drop 4 lines.
Indent.

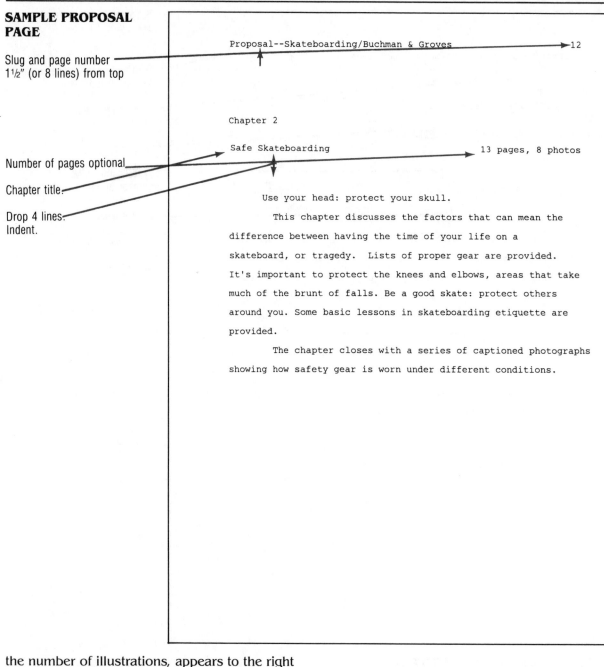

```
          Proposal--Skateboarding/Buchman & Groves                    12



          Chapter 2

          Safe Skateboarding                          13 pages, 8 photos


               Use your head: protect your skull.

                    This chapter discusses the factors that can mean the

               difference between having the time of your life on a

               skateboard, or tragedy.  Lists of proper gear are provided.

               It's important to protect the knees and elbows, areas that take

               much of the brunt of falls. Be a good skate: protect others

               around you. Some basic lessons in skateboarding etiquette are

               provided.

                    The chapter closes with a series of captioned photographs

               showing how safety gear is worn under different conditions.
```

the number of illustrations, appears to the right of the chapter number. You may have to change this when you work on the book. Remember: We said outlines should be flexible; your editor will understand these changes as the book progresses.

How detailed would an unstripped version be? We suggest you look at the sample provided in Michael Larsen's book *How to Write a Book Proposal* (Writer's Digest Books), which we've cited several times in this book.

SAMPLE PROPOSAL PAGE

Skateboarding/Buchman & Groves   20

PART II: NATIONAL COMPETITIONS

Chapter 4

Skateboarding for Fun and Profit   10 pages, 4 photos

    Skateboarding competitions are increasing across the
United States and Canada. Prizes vary from loving cups to
money and other valuables. Techniques, such as perfecting the
Aerial Move, and other important competitive skills are
discussed. Illustrations accompany the discussions.

Slug and page number
1½" from top

Drop 4 lines.

In CAPS

Drop 2 lines.

Drop 2 lines.

Drop 4 lines.

Double-space.

**SAMPLE PROPOSAL
PAGE**—Appendix

Slug and page number
1½″ from top of page

Drop 4 lines.

Drop 2 lines.
Indent,
double-space.

List each item in a separate
paragraph.

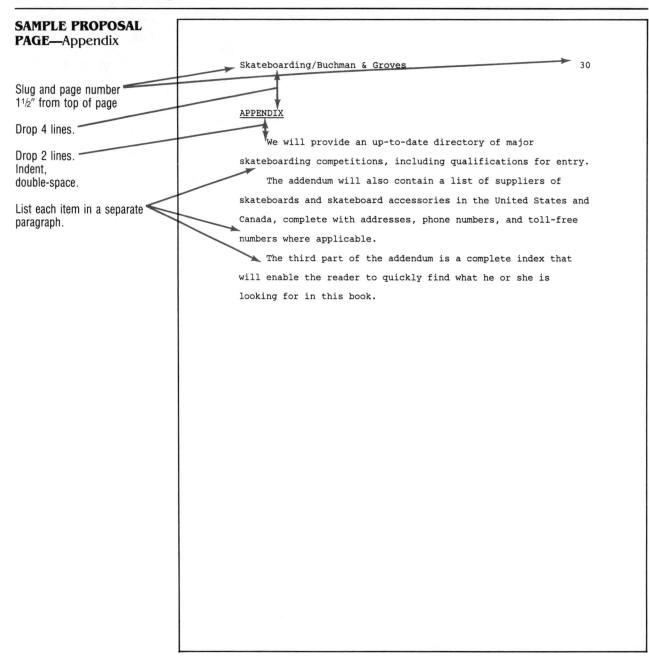

Skateboarding/Buchman & Groves   30

APPENDIX

We will provide an up-to-date directory of major
skateboarding competitions, including qualifications for entry.
    The addendum will also contain a list of suppliers of
skateboards and skateboard accessories in the United States and
Canada, complete with addresses, phone numbers, and toll-free
numbers where applicable.
    The third part of the addendum is a complete index that
will enable the reader to quickly find what he or she is
looking for in this book.

SAMPLE CHAPTERS

When submitting sample chapters for a *nonfiction* book, it isn't necessary to send along sequential chapters (the practice generally followed with fiction work, in which the story follows in a certain order). The chapters you send, however, should show how well you write and how clearly you make your points.

In our proposal for our hypothetical book, we chose Chapter 1 because it is a basic introduction to skateboarding information. In an actual nonfiction proposal you would send at least two chapters (not necessarily consecutive). In choosing them try to give the editor a clear idea of the diversity of material in the book.

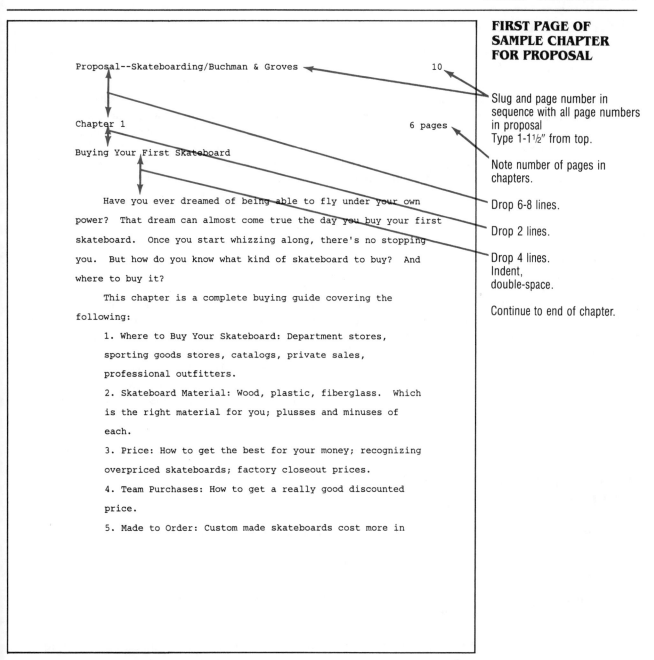

**FIRST PAGE OF
SAMPLE CHAPTER
FOR PROPOSAL**

Proposal--Skateboarding/Buchman & Groves   10

Slug and page number in
sequence with all page numbers
in proposal
Type 1-1½" from top.

Chapter 1   6 pages

Note number of pages in
chapters.

Buying Your First Skateboard

Drop 6-8 lines.

Drop 2 lines.

Drop 4 lines.
Indent,
double-space.

Continue to end of chapter.

Have you ever dreamed of being able to fly under your own
power? That dream can almost come true the day you buy your first
skateboard. Once you start whizzing along, there's no stopping
you. But how do you know what kind of skateboard to buy? And
where to buy it?

This chapter is a complete buying guide covering the
following:

1. Where to Buy Your Skateboard: Department stores,
sporting goods stores, catalogs, private sales,
professional outfitters.

2. Skateboard Material: Wood, plastic, fiberglass. Which
is the right material for you; plusses and minuses of
each.

3. Price: How to get the best for your money; recognizing
overpriced skateboards; factory closeout prices.

4. Team Purchases: How to get a really good discounted
price.

5. Made to Order: Custom made skateboards cost more in

The Proposal Numbers Game

When you submit sample chapters for a proposal, the pages are numbered in the same sequence; for example, if the first page of the first sample chapter follows page 15 in the proposal, then the first page of the chapter would be page 16; if the chapter ends at page 22, the first page of the following sample chapter would be page 23, and so on.

Authors' Tip: When we work on a manuscript, particularly a nonfiction book, we rarely work from page 1 to "the end" in sequence. Therefore, we pencil in page numbers sequentially in each chapter. When the final draft of the manuscript is finished, we fit the chapters in where they belong and then repaginate accordingly.

So, when you submit your sample chapters, which are numbered in the proposal's page order, be sure you pencil in the page numbers per chapter on copies you keep. Remember: They will be your *working copies.*

PROPOSAL ENDNOTES

Now that your nonfiction book proposal is finished, there are still a few steps you should follow.

First: Check to see that all pages are numbered correctly. This is a good opportunity to discover any missing material.

Second: Never staple or punch holes in your material. Use a large paper clip, or slip the pages into a binder, preferably one with a clear plastic cover.

Third: Mail your proposal in a 9x12 envelope. If your proposal has six or fewer pages, you can mail it, folded once, in a 6x9 envelope.

Fourth: Use your postal scale before affixing postage, or check the postage rate guide on page 150, which will give you postage rates according to the number of pages you are sending.

The *Proposal Worksheet* that appears in Et Cetera will help you to organize your thoughts as you prepare your proposal. You'll find it on page 185.

FRONT MATTER

Once your book is accepted, you may have to present the various items normally found in the front of a finished book, called *front matter*. Two items are absolutely required: a manuscript title page as well as the table of contents (also called *contents*). But *you* the author are free to choose whether or not you will include a dedication, foreword, preface, acknowledgments, or special quotes called an *inscription* or *epigraph*. However, if your book includes tables or illustrations, you will need to list them in the section of the front matter called *list of tables* or *list of illustrations*. Usually, front matter is typed after the entire manuscript is finished. The pages are not formally numbered, but when you submit them you may want to lightly pencil in page numbers after page one. Your editor adds the publication page numbers later.

AT-A-GLANCE GUIDE TO FRONT MATTER

Title Page	See sample, page 31. Center title in middle of page.
	Do not use a page number.
Author's name	Type author's name, address, and phone number in upper left-hand corner.
Agent's name	If relevant, type name, address, and phone number several spaces under author's name, or in lower right-hand corner of the page.
Approximate word count	Type approximate number of words (rounded off) in right-hand corner, on the same line with name.
Title	Use initial caps for each word except articles, conjunctions, and prepositions. (Exception: prepositions over five letters, such as *Without* or *Between*.) Also use initial caps for words following a semi-colon or colon.
Sample	*The Story of Civilization: Part IV*

Table of Contents	See sample, pages 32-33.
	There are four possible styles to preparation—two main styles are illustrated.
	Center the heading *Table of Contents* (or *Contents*) 2 inches or 12 lines from top of page.
	Allow 6 lines or at least 1 inch at the bottom of the page.
	Do not repeat title or type in *continued* if the contents takes up more than one page.

Vertical Spacing

Triple-space	Triple-space between title and first entry.
	Triple-space after an entry and a part (Part I, Part II, etc.).
Double-space	Double-space between part and following entry.
	Double-space between chapter headings and first entry of a subheading.
Single-space	Single-space between individual subheadings.

Runover Lines

Heading	If heading runs over, divide and align with the preceding line.
Heading of a part	The heading of a part is centered; thus, the runover lines are also centered.
Subheading	If subheading has runover lines, indent 3 spaces on next line.
Lists of Illustrations	Needed only if you include illustrations.
	Separate page; no numbers.
	Type each list separately.
	Center. Drop 3 inches or 18 spaces from top of page. Type, in upper and lower case: *List of Illustrations* or *Index of Illustrations*.
	See illustration section, page 172, for code and numbering instructions.
Lists of Tables	Needed only if you include tables.
	Separate page; no numbers. Type each list separately. See sample, page 36.
	Center. Drop 3 inches or 18 spaces from top of page. Capitalize as in a title (upper and lower case).

These items are optional:

Dedication Page	Use separate page. Do not number. Do not type the word *Dedication;* instead begin with either the word *To* or the word *For.*
	Center material on the page. Capitalize the first letter in proper nouns, as in a sentence. See sample, page 37.
Epigraph or Inscription	An *epigraph* or *inscription* is a quotation instead of a dedication at the beginning of either a fiction or nonfiction book. The second kind of epigraph is a quotation at the beginning of a chapter. Each is typed in a different way. Do not type the heading *Epigraph* or *Inscription;* start with the quote.
Beginning of book	Type on separate page. Do not number. Center on page.
	At end of quote, type author's name and title of work, and line up flush right with the longest line of quote.
Head of chapter(s)	Indent as in paragraph, but use block format. Place author's name as above. See sample, page 38.
Foreword	Separate pages—usually between two and four. Usually written by a known expert other than the author. See sample, page 39.
	Type and center the word *Foreword* 3 inches or eighteen spaces from top of page.
	Skip four spaces from *Foreword* to first line of text.
	At end of foreword, skip four lines, type the author's name and title flush right. Type author's affiliation flush left, same line.
Preface	If you want to explain the scope, background, reasons, and purpose of the book, and acknowledge certain research and institution help, it goes into the preface. If you prefer, skip the preface for acknowledgments.
	Drop down 3 inches or 18 spaces from top of page. Center. In caps, type PREFACE.
End of preface	Type month and year flush left. If you add the city and state, also type flush left.
	Type your name and affiliation flush right. See sample, page 40.

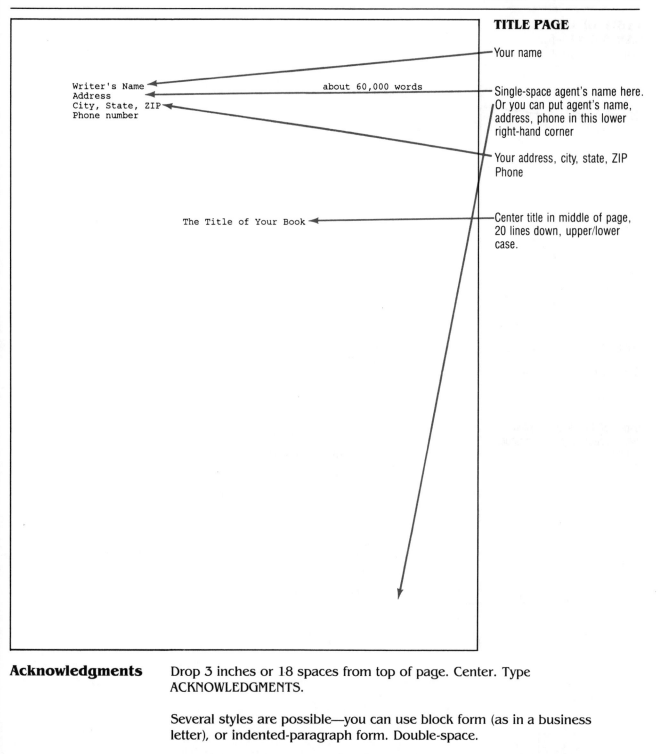

TITLE PAGE

Your name

Writer's Name
Address
City, State, ZIP
Phone number

about 60,000 words

Single-space agent's name here.
Or you can put agent's name,
address, phone in this lower
right-hand corner

Your address, city, state, ZIP
Phone

The Title of Your Book

Center title in middle of page,
20 lines down, upper/lower
case.

Acknowledgments   Drop 3 inches or 18 spaces from top of page. Center. Type
ACKNOWLEDGMENTS.

Several styles are possible—you can use block form (as in a business
letter), or indented-paragraph form. Double-space.

End acknowledgments by skipping several lines. Type your name and
affiliation flush right. Type the month and year and (optional) city and
state, flush left. See sample, page 41.

**TABLE OF CONTENTS
SAMPLE #1**—for
nonfiction book

Slug

No page number

Dreamsleep/Bellows

Centered

Drop 3 lines.

Double-space

Capitalize first letter of each
word except prepositions under
5 letters.

Table of Contents

1-1½" from bottom of page

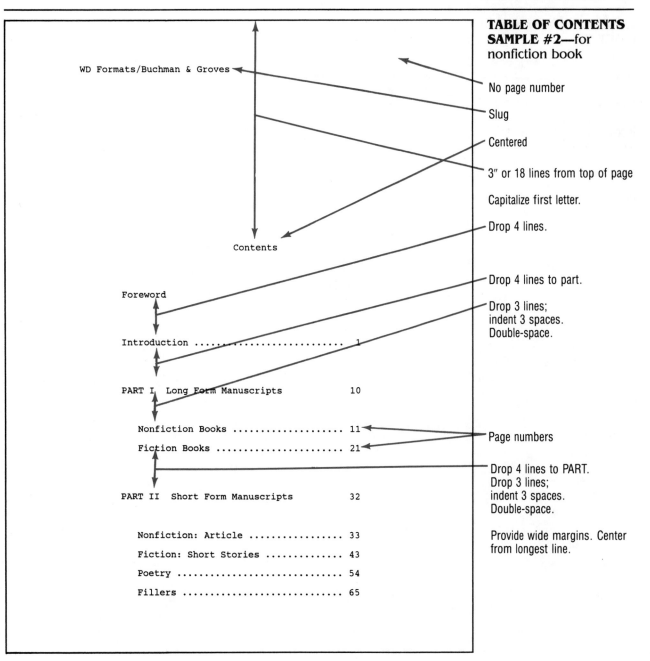

TABLE OF CONTENTS SAMPLE #2—for nonfiction book

No page number

Slug

Centered

3″ or 18 lines from top of page

Capitalize first letter.

Drop 4 lines.

Drop 4 lines to part.

Drop 3 lines; indent 3 spaces. Double-space.

Page numbers

Drop 4 lines to PART. Drop 3 lines; indent 3 spaces. Double-space.

Provide wide margins. Center from longest line.

**TABLE OF CONTENTS
(PAGE 2)**

Slug

Do not number.

If continued to next page, do
not type word *Contents*.

Double-space.

Drop 4 lines between PARTS.

WD Formats/Buchman & Groves

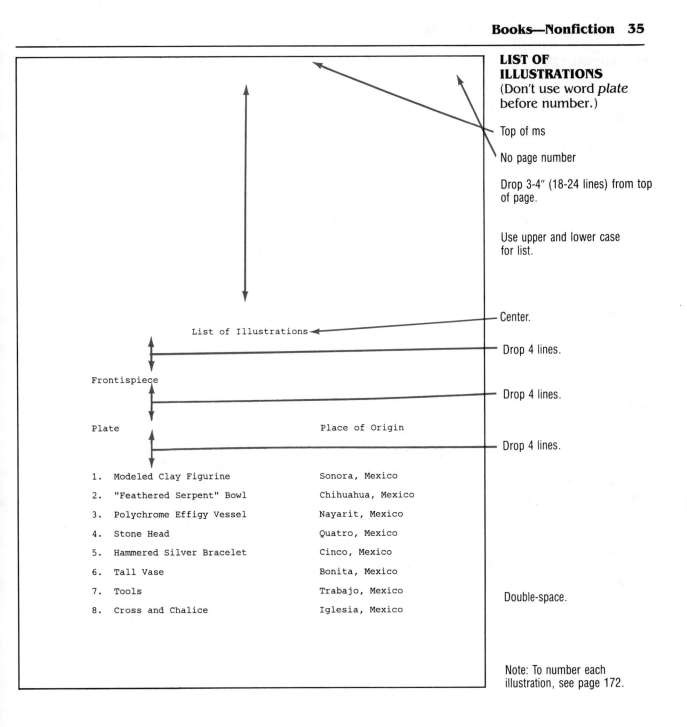

LIST OF ILLUSTRATIONS
(Don't use word *plate* before number.)

Top of ms

No page number

Drop 3-4″ (18-24 lines) from top of page.

Use upper and lower case for list.

Center.

Drop 4 lines.

Drop 4 lines.

Drop 4 lines.

List of Illustrations

Frontispiece

Plate		Place of Origin
1.	Modeled Clay Figurine	Sonora, Mexico
2.	"Feathered Serpent" Bowl	Chihuahua, Mexico
3.	Polychrome Effigy Vessel	Nayarit, Mexico
4.	Stone Head	Quatro, Mexico
5.	Hammered Silver Bracelet	Cinco, Mexico
6.	Tall Vase	Bonita, Mexico
7.	Tools	Trabajo, Mexico
8.	Cross and Chalice	Iglesia, Mexico

Double-space.

Note: To number each illustration, see page 172.

LIST OF TABLES

Slug

No page number

Drop about 3″ or 18 spaces.

Center, upper and lower case.

Drop 4 lines.

Number each table in sequence.

Double-space.
Single-space, indent second line 3 spaces.

Drop 4 lines between parts.

Center.

Drop 3 lines to entry.

Indent second line.
Double-space between entries.

Drop 4 lines between last entry and new part.

Center.

Page number

Foods/Mark

List of Tables

1.	Composition of foods, 100 grams edible portion.	6
2.	Nutrients in the edible portion of 1 pound of food as purchased	68
3.	Selected fatty acids in foods	122
4.	Cholesterol content of foods	146
5.	Magnesium content of foods	147

Appendix A

6.	Data used for calculating energy values of foods or food groups by the Atwater System	160
7.	Available energy from different types of diets	161

Appendix B

8.	Factors for calculating protein from nitrogen content of food	161
9.	Preformed niacin and potential niacin equivalents	169
10.	Standards for enrichment	171

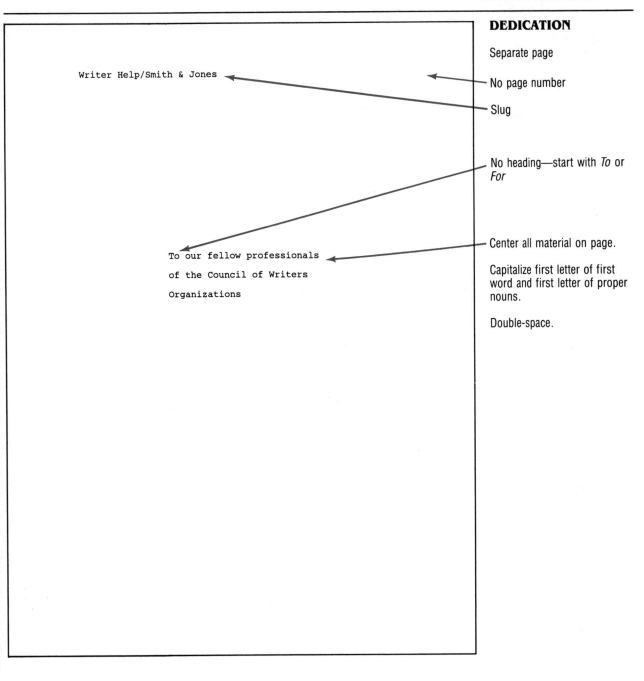

DEDICATION

Separate page

No page number

Slug

No heading—start with *To* or *For*

Center all material on page.

Capitalize first letter of first word and first letter of proper nouns.

Double-space.

EPIGRAPH OR INSCRIPTION
(Head of chapter)

Slug

No page number

Drop 18 lines.

Indent.

Double-space.

Drop 2 lines—author and source ends flush right with longest line.

Drop 4-6 lines for chapter headings; center.

Drop 2 lines for chapter title.

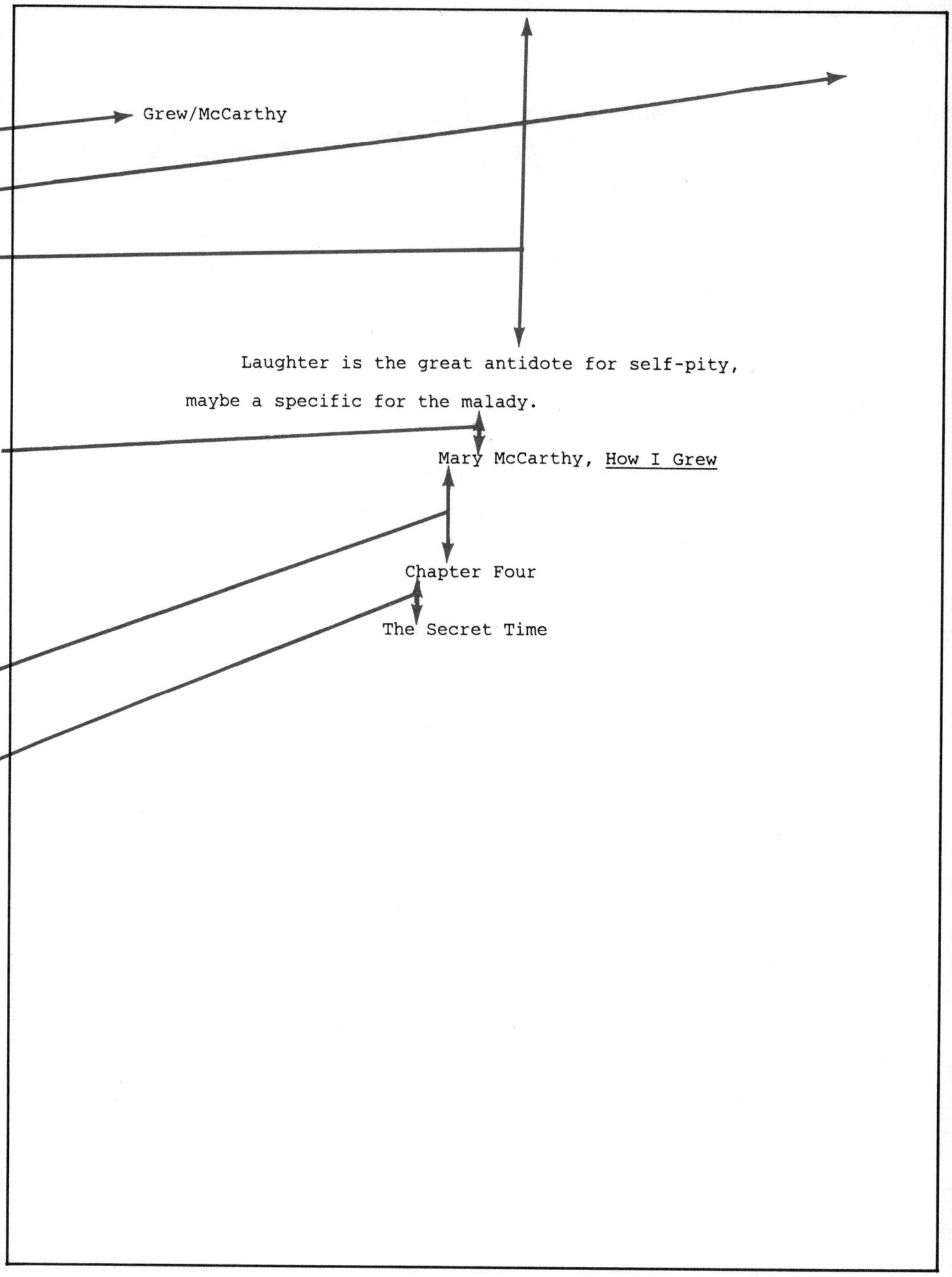

Grew/McCarthy

Laughter is the great antidote for self-pity,

maybe a specific for the malady.

Mary McCarthy, _How I Grew_

Chapter Four

The Secret Time

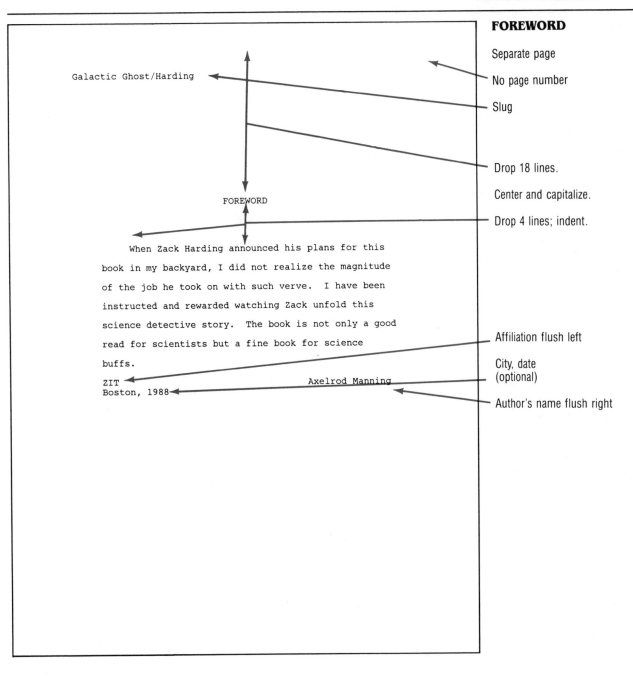

Galactic Ghost/Harding

FOREWORD

    When Zack Harding announced his plans for this
book in my backyard, I did not realize the magnitude
of the job he took on with such verve. I have been
instructed and rewarded watching Zack unfold this
science detective story. The book is not only a good
read for scientists but a fine book for science
buffs.

ZIT
Boston, 1988   Axelrod Manning

FOREWORD

Separate page

No page number

Slug

Drop 18 lines.

Center and capitalize.

Drop 4 lines; indent.

Affiliation flush left

City, date
(optional)

Author's name flush right

PREFACE

Separate page

No page number ─────────────

Slug ─────────────

Drop 18 lines from top on
separate page.

Center;
capitalize.

Drop 4 spaces to text.
Indent first line of each
paragraph.

Drop 2 lines from text;
place and date flush left

Drop 2 lines from text;
author's initials or full name
flush right

```
                              Rueful Murders/Wright




                                 PREFACE

                 This book was born out of my fascination with an

            old murder story that I read aloud as a child, and

            which has haunted me through the years.  I am grateful

            to the people at the Paris Gazette for providing me with

            background material to the case, and to the members of

            the police departments of Paris, France for giving me

            access to their files on this case.

            Toonerville, Texas                              I.W.
            December, 1989
```

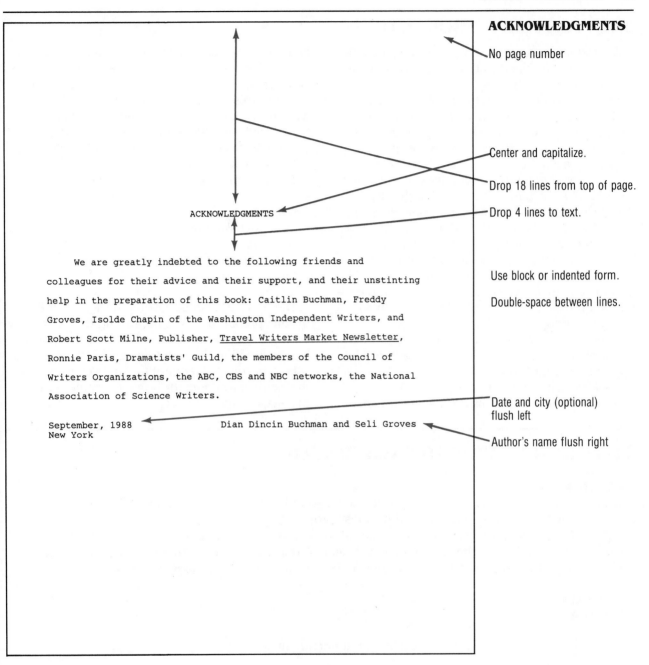

ACKNOWLEDGMENTS

No page number

ACKNOWLEDGMENTS

Center and capitalize.

Drop 18 lines from top of page.

Drop 4 lines to text.

We are greatly indebted to the following friends and colleagues for their advice and their support, and their unstinting help in the preparation of this book: Caitlin Buchman, Freddy Groves, Isolde Chapin of the Washington Independent Writers, and Robert Scott Milne, Publisher, <u>Travel Writers Market Newsletter</u>, Ronnie Paris, Dramatists' Guild, the members of the Council of Writers Organizations, the ABC, CBS and NBC networks, the National Association of Science Writers.

Use block or indented form.

Double-space between lines.

September, 1988
New York

Dian Dincin Buchman and Seli Groves

Date and city (optional) flush left

Author's name flush right

BACK MATTER: INTRODUCTION

The following guides show you how to type the various material found in the *back matter* section of most nonfiction books.

Back matter appears in the published book after the basic book is completed. It can be best compared to a series of *postscripts;* additional and valuable information that is better presented separately from the running text. The different types of back matter have identities of their own: for example, the appendix, the bibliography, etc.

The value of a well-researched book is enhanced with its back-matter additions. Therefore, it's a good idea, when you come up with an idea for a book, to be prepared not only to research the material that will go between page 1 and THE END of your manuscript, but also to assemble information that will be suitable for insertion as back-matter copy.

Again, keep in mind that as with the *front matter,* some of the back matter may or may not be required for your book.

What you will see in the pages ahead are an At-a-Glance Guide followed by discussions of each type of back-matter section; we will tell you how it's used in the book and how it's typed by you or your typist. (We hope these discussions will help you find this sometimes-puzzling part of your work much easier than you thought. Through them, we have attempted to do everything short of coming over to construct the back matter ourselves on your typewriter or word processor.)

The elements discussed—and diagrammed— are:

Endnotes
Appendix (Appendices)
Glossary
List of Abbreviations
Bibliography
Indexes

The index is also part of the back matter but is usually prepared by the publishing house. However, it's a good idea to learn how to do indexes, so it is included in the At-a-Glance Guide. Some publishers permit (or require) the authors to prepare their own. Programs for home computers make this step faster than ever.

AT-A-GLANCE GUIDE TO BACK MATTER

Endnotes

What are endnotes? Endnotes are used for documentation of some book manuscripts, but are mostly needed in reports, journals, and business proposals.

Styles of presentation vary. List notes either at the end of the document or at the end of each chapter. (Check with publisher for guidelines.) Keep in mind that some camera-ready manuscripts often require single-spaced notes at the *foot* of the page. (See sample, page 47.)

If no special
instructions:

Short document	Group notes at end of document.
Longer document	Group notes at end of each chapter.
Presentation	Start notes on separate page.
	Drop 2 inches or 12 spaces from top of page and, for shorter document, type *Notes.* For longer document, type *Notes to Chapter 10,* or *Notes to Section One,* etc.
Typing author's name	Drop 3 lines. Start typing notes. Type author's name in normal sequence, first name first (Seli Groves, Dian Dincin Buchman).

Between notes	Skip one line between each note. However, some journals require double-spacing between notes.
Numbering of pages	*Short Document:* Number the pages in sequence at end of document. *Long Document:* Number the pages in sequence after end of each chapter, or end of book after last page of appendix.

Appendix

This is a useful section with material related to the text but not entirely suitable for inclusion in it. Possible items to go in an appendix: documents, tables, long case studies, schedules, forms, some illustrative material. (See sample, page 48.)

If you have more than one category	Divide into categories and assign a letter or number system such as Appendix 1, Appendix 2, etc.; or, Appendix A, Appendix B, etc.
Numbering if more than one in a category	Number each category in sequence as: 1:1, 1:2, 1:3, or A:1, A:2, A:3, depending on whether you choose a number or letter style.
More than one appendix	For more than one appendix, give each a descriptive title. Number in same way as above.
Numbering pages	In sequence with the rest of the book, e.g., 145, 146, 147.
Presentation	Drop 3 inches or 18 lines from top of page. Type *Appendix*. Center on page. Drop 4 lines to first word of text.
Typing	Type tables and illustrations and most data as in main text. Exceptions: Documents and case studies are often typed in single spacing; however, explanations, methods, and procedures are double-spaced.

Glossary

A glossary alphabetically lists and defines technical and foreign words or phrases. (See samples, pages 49, 50.)

Presentation	Alphabetize as in dictionary.
	Begin each word on a separate line.
	Type word flush with left margin.
	Follow with comma or colon, then definition or translation.
	Indent all runover (long) lines three spaces.
	Single-space each entry.
	Double-space between entries.
	If definitions consist of a sentence or more, end each entry with a period.
	Use no final punctuation if only words or phrases.

List of Abbreviations

Such a list is needed only if you have devised arbitrary abbreviations for footnotes or elsewhere, e.g.:

f—feminine	Ger—German	It—Italian
Fr—French	Gk—Greek	L—Latin

Generally, it is wise to avoid abbreviations in the text, except in scientific and technical writing. A safe rule is to use only a few standard abbreviations. (See sample, page 51.)

Be consistent in your usage

Don't abbreviate addresses. Spell out *Avenue, Place, Street, Boulevard.*

Don't put periods in common abbreviations such as MGM, FBI, PTA, NBC, UN, CIA, CBS, ABC, NY, DC

Exceptions: a.m., p.m., i.e., e.g., C.O.D., A.D., B.C.

Presentation

Alphabetize each list by the abbreviation, not the fully spelled-out form.

Begin each abbreviation on a separate line.

Type each abbreviation flush left with margin.

Follow abbreviation with comma or colon and definition.

Indent runover lines three spaces.

Single-space each entry.

Double-space between entries.

Use no formal punctuation for words or phrases. However, if definition is more than one sentence, use periods after each one.

Bibliography

A bibliography is a list of the works cited in a manuscript. A less formal heading is "Works Consulted" or "Works Cited." (See sample, page 52.)

Presentation

List alphabetically by author, last name first, e.g., Gowers, Ernest. Add a period after the author's name.

Divide into categories if bibliography is extensive.

Drop 3 inches or 18 spaces from top of page; type and center *Bibliography* or *Works Cited* or *Works Consulted.*

Skip 4 spaces to text.

Type flush with left-hand margin.

If entry runs over the line, indent the subsequent lines five spaces.

Use single-spacing in typing entry.

Double-space between entries.

If more than one author: First author—give last name first. Second author and all other authors—give first name first (e.g., Buchman, Dian Dincin, Seli Groves).

Underline the title of the book.

Type city (and state) of publication, publisher, and date (e.g., New York: Wise & Co., 1939).

Type colon before subtitle (e.g., *Herbal Medicine: The Natural Way to Get Well and Stay Well*).

Put a period at the end of each entry.

Do not number the entries.

Index

The index is the key to the pertinent data in your book. Usually the indexing is turned over to a professional indexer. The cost of this index is usually charged against your advance and royalty account. If your book is scholarly or complex you may want to do your own index. Discuss this with your editor. In addition to the following general overview, also refer to these reference manuals: *The Chicago Manual of Style*, University of Chicago Press; Sina Spiker, *Indexing Your Book: A Practical Guide For Authors*, University of Wisconsin Press; Ruth Candy Cross, *Indexing Books*, The Word Guild; Robert L. Collison, *Indexes and Indexing*, John de Graff, Inc.

Entries	How many you include depends on the nature of the work, space allotted to this index, and publisher's guidelines. The usual formula is about five index lines for each text page.
Question to ask	Ask yourself, "How will my readers look this up?" The Adelle Davis books are an excellent example of useful indexes. Also see Theodore M. Bernstein's *Reverse Dictionary* (Times Books) for a fresh approach to finding words.
Cards	Professional indexers use 3x5 index cards or (preferably) long strips of attached perforated card stock for entries (these can be run through the typewriter or computer).
When to index	Arrange with your publisher. Obviously, it has to be after the book has been arranged in pages the way it will appear in print. These are often called "page proofs."
When page proofs arrive	Cut the sheets into manageable pages. Give the page proofs your first read. Underline key words and phrases. In the margin, pencil in possible heads. At this stage include more rather than less—later it will help you to locate hard to find items (and you can always eliminate and pare down).
How to type	Put one heading (and page number) per card.

More than one index	If you have a complex project with many names, you may want to develop two indexes: one of *persons* in the book, the other of *subjects and proper names* other than persons. It is safer to do each index separately. Later you will combine them in alphabetical order.
Alphabetizing systems	1. Temporarily keep cards in page-number order until you work through the entire book. Then alphabetize all at once. (This is easier and faster for the novice indexer.) OR 2. Alphabetize as you go along. (This makes it easier to add fresh references and subheads as well as compress, combine entries, and add items as you go along.) Both systems are used by professionals.
Cross reference	Add cross references (and page numbers) for important data. When there are a great many cross references you can type: *See,* or *See Also.*
Typing	Use 20-pound bond, 8½"x11" white paper. Type: INDEX about ⅓ of the way (or 20 lines) down the page. Retype complete alphabetical listings. Double space items. Type in one-column format. Allow wide margins on sides, top and bottom for editorial and designer notations. Triple-space between each alphabetical section. Submit typed version only—hold on to alphabetized cards until book is printed.
Punctuation	Follow publisher's style sheet or guidelines for special punctuation and capitalization instructions. Use no punctuation at the end of an entry.
Not indexed	Preliminary material such as the dedication, inscription (epigraph), foreword, preface, table of contents, lists of illustrations and tables are not indexed. Specific illustrations may be indexed if it contributes to the use of the book. Generally back matter is not indexed. However, if your appendix contains material not in the text, it should be indexed. For additional material consult indexing texts.

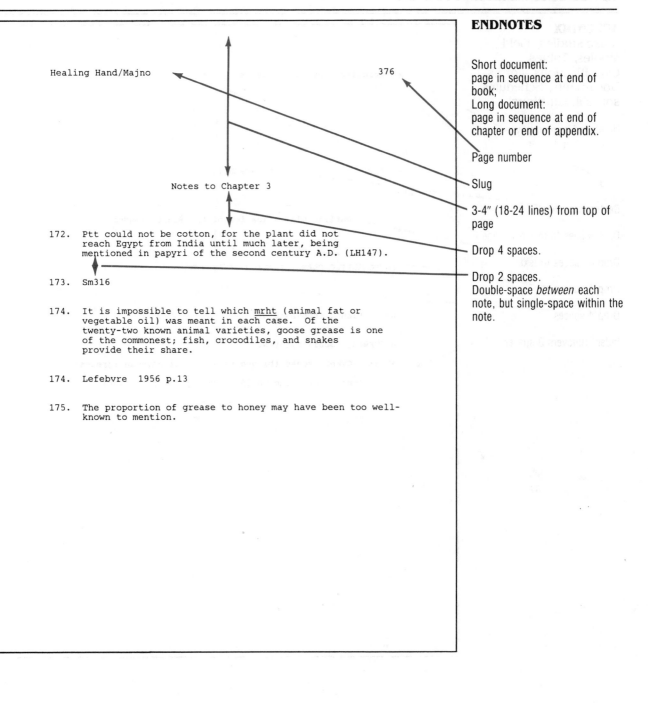

Healing Hand/Majno

376

Notes to Chapter 3

172. Ptt could not be cotton, for the plant did not reach Egypt from India until much later, being mentioned in papyri of the second century A.D. (LH147).

173. Sm316

174. It is impossible to tell which mrht (animal fat or vegetable oil) was meant in each case. Of the twenty-two known animal varieties, goose grease is one of the commonest; fish, crocodiles, and snakes provide their share.

174. Lefebvre 1956 p.13

175. The proportion of grease to honey may have been too well-known to mention.

Short document:
page in sequence at end of book;
Long document:
page in sequence at end of chapter or end of appendix.

Page number

Slug

3-4″ (18-24 lines) from top of page

Drop 4 spaces.

Drop 2 spaces.
Double-space *between* each note, but single-space within the note.

APPENDIX
(Case studies, Field
studies, Tables,
Classifications, Forms,
Documents, Schedules,
some illustrations)

Numbered sequentially

Slug

Center; capitalize.

Drop 8 lines from top of page.

Drop 4 spaces to text.

Drop 4 spaces.

Drop 4 spaces.

Indent runovers 3 spaces.

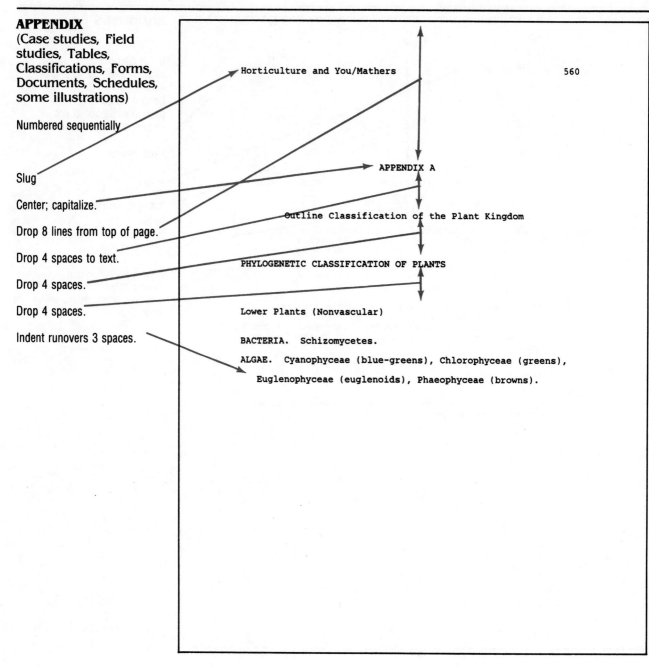

Horticulture and You/Mathers   560

APPENDIX A

Outline Classification of the Plant Kingdom

PHYLOGENETIC CLASSIFICATION OF PLANTS

Lower Plants (Nonvascular)

BACTERIA. Schizomycetes.

ALGAE. Cyanophyceae (blue-greens), Chlorophyceae (greens),
      Euglenophyceae (euglenoids), Phaeophyceae (browns).

GLOSSARY

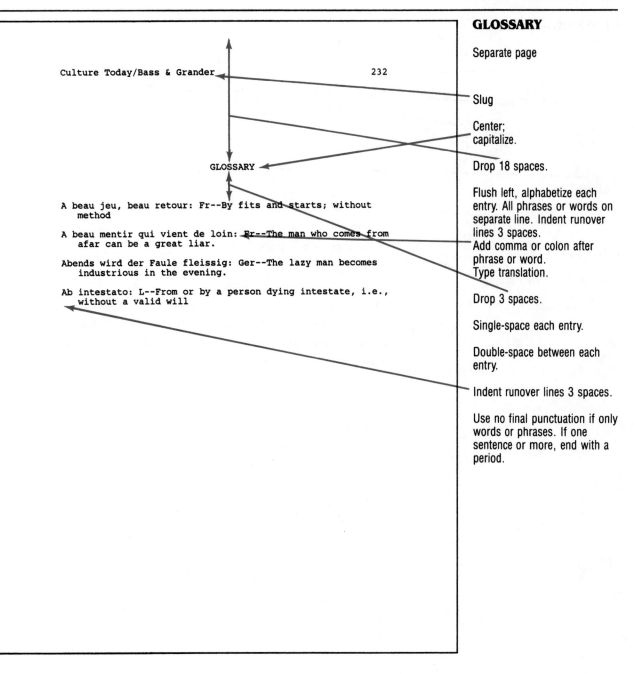

Separate page

Slug

Center;
capitalize.

Drop 18 spaces.

Flush left, alphabetize each entry. All phrases or words on separate line. Indent runover lines 3 spaces.

Add comma or colon after phrase or word.

Type translation.

Drop 3 spaces.

Single-space each entry.

Double-space between each entry.

Indent runover lines 3 spaces.

Use no final punctuation if only words or phrases. If one sentence or more, end with a period.

Culture Today/Bass & Grander   232

GLOSSARY

A beau jeu, beau retour: Fr--By fits and starts; without method

A beau mentir qui vient de loin: Fr--The man who comes from afar can be a great liar.

Abends wird der Faule fleissig: Ger--The lazy man becomes industrious in the evening.

Ab intestato: L--From or by a person dying intestate, i.e., without a valid will

GLOSSARY—Alternate Style

Slug —————————→ Scientific Gardening/Trawell ———————————————→ 115

Drop 3-4″ from top of page. ———

Page numbered sequentially with book manuscript

Center;————————————————————————→ GLOSSARY
capitalize.

Flush left ——————————————————→ Achene: A small, dry, hard, nonsplitting fruit with one seed

Alphabetize each entry. ————→ Alien: Foreign, but successfully established; in our area by

Indent runover lines 3 spaces. ———→   man, or as an escape

No final punctuation

Alternate (leaves, etc.): Not opposite each other

Bloom: A waxy or whitish coating on stem, leaf, or fruit

Calyz: The outer circle of floral leaves (sepals): usually

    green, sometimes like petals; may be separate or joined

Drupe: A fleshy fruit with a hard nut or stone (as a cherry)

Herbs: Fleshy, nonwoody plants

LIST OF ABBREVIATIONS

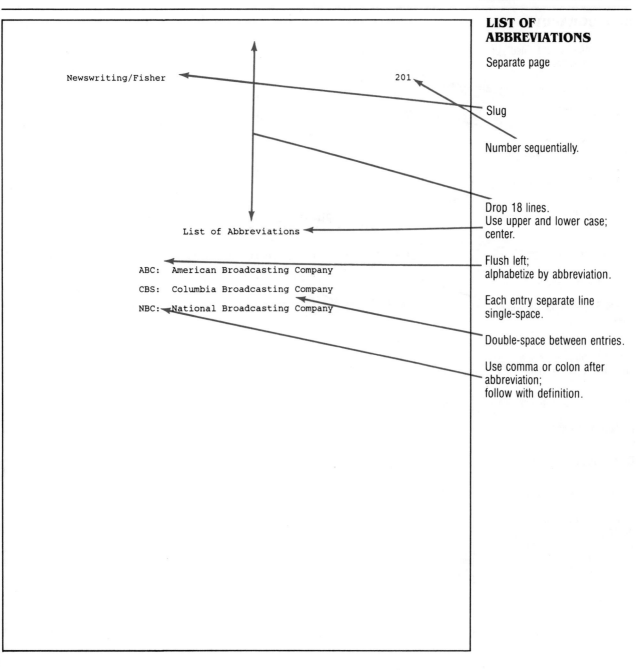

Newswriting/Fisher

201

List of Abbreviations

ABC: American Broadcasting Company

CBS: Columbia Broadcasting Company

NBC: National Broadcasting Company

Separate page

Slug

Number sequentially.

Drop 18 lines.
Use upper and lower case;
center.

Flush left;
alphabetize by abbreviation.

Each entry separate line
single-space.

Double-space between entries.

Use comma or colon after
abbreviation;
follow with definition.

BIBLIOGRAPHY

Also can use "Works Cited" or "Works Consulted"

Number in sequence

Slug

Drop 18 lines; center, upper and lower case.

Flush with left-hand margin

List alphabetically by author, last name first.

Period after author

Colon before subtitle

Indent 5 spaces for runover lines.

City of publication, colon, publisher, comma, date

Double-space between entries.

Underline title of book.

Do not number entries.

Single-space each entry.

If more than one author: first author, give last name first. Second author and all other authors, give first name first.

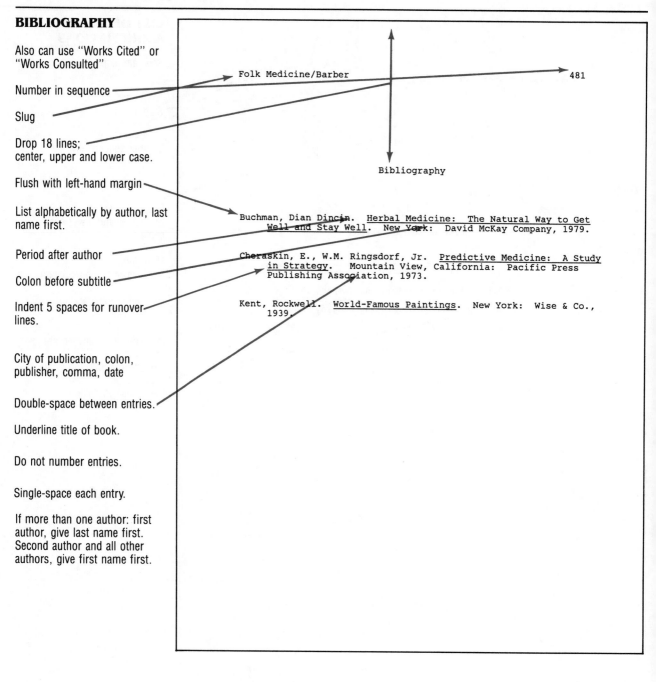

```
Folk Medicine/Barber                                            481



                              Bibliography



Buchman, Dian Dincin.  Herbal Medicine:  The Natural Way to Get
       Well and Stay Well.  New York:  David McKay Company, 1979.

Cheraskin, E., W.M. Ringsdorf, Jr.  Predictive Medicine:  A Study
       in Strategy.  Mountain View, California:  Pacific Press
       Publishing Association, 1973.

Kent, Rockwell.  World-Famous Paintings.  New York:  Wise & Co.,
       1939.
```

FICTION

Writing fiction, says Mary Higgins Clark, author of many bestsellers, including *Stillwatch* and *Weep No More, My Lady*, is a matter of taking a real situation and asking "What if . . ." or "Suppose . . . ." The writer then tells the story that evolves from that premise.

This is true for every fiction medium, including science fiction, romance, mystery, suspense, etc., and for every fiction format, including short stories, anthologies, novels, and novellas.

What is also true for every fiction medium is that the ultimate sale of the work depends on how good it is. The work speaks for itself.

Form

However, while the content may sell the novel or the short story, the manuscript in which it is presented for sale is expected to be in a generally accepted format that most editors prefer to work with.

This chapter of long-form fiction (novels and novellas) shows how to prepare the formats that are most often preferred by editors who buy fiction.

Among the forms discussed in this section are query letters, proposals, outlines, manuscript pages, and cover letters. Samples of each format will be presented. Line spacing, margins, and placement of elements on each page will be shown and diagrammed to provide precise guides to preparation. In addition, you'll want to refer to the At-a-Glance Guide to Typing Manuscript Pages, pages 2-5, 66, 167-68, and the At-a-Glance Guide to Front Matter in Novels, page 71.

Submission

Once the work is complete, it needs to be sent out. This section provides information on how to prepare your fiction to mail, or otherwise deliver, to a book publisher. (Refer to pages 147-150 in the Mailing section.)

Making Contact

To query or not to query? No wonder so many fiction writers seem to be in a quandary about queries. Some people say, "Always query"; others say, "Just send the manuscript in with a cover letter."

This section will discuss the query question in detail.

NOVELS AND NOVELLAS

This section opens with a complete look at manuscript preparation for novels and novellas. In some instances, information given in one part will overlap with information in another part. And in some cases, we'll refer you to other parts of the book.

In Quest of Sales

The selling of a novel or a novella (the dictionary defines *novella* as a short prose form, often with a specific moral to point out) depends basically on the quality of the work. But don't try to use that argument to sell a sloppily prepared manuscript that screams "AMATEUR!" even before anyone reads the first paragraph. By the time you reach the point at which you feel you can sell your written work, it's expected that you have some knowledge of how to present it.

That goes for the presubmission presentation of your idea as well.

Do you send a query letter first—as your nonfiction writing colleague generally does?

Do you send a proposal? An outline? If so, how detailed is your outline?

Do you need to send sample chapters? If so, how many? In sequence or not?

Do you send a completed manuscript and skip the proposal step altogether?

Querying Fiction Editors

Authors of novels are more likely to query editors than are writers of short stories. (Indeed, the usual practice for magazine editors is to work with a complete short story submitted without a previous query.)

It's also a good idea for a new writer to query an editor first. BUT . . . before you send out a query, you should have your proposal and at least three sequential chapters of your novel ready to submit, in case your query strikes a responsive note. It's an even better idea to have your full manuscript ready to go, particularly if you are a new or (so far) relatively unknown writer.

First, determine which publishers you want to contact. (*Fiction Writer's Market* can provide information on publishing houses specializing in fiction.) Direct your letter to a specific editor at the house. (You can call to find out the names of editors in the various departments if no names are given.)

Determine what you want to say in the letter. The following is a guide to what your query might contain in descending order of priority:

1. Introduce yourself. (You want them to know you're a writer, not someone trying to sell office supplies.)

2. Describe your book. What type of book is it: romance, mystery, historical novel, suspense? Give a brief overview of what the book is about, e.g., if you were the author of *The Thorn Birds* you might say: "My book is set in Australia and deals with a family over several generations, from the time they first settle in Australia in the early nineteenth century on through the present day. Some of the situations they encounter include coping with natural disasters such as fires and storms, passionate entanglements, including a forbidden love affair between a headstrong young woman and a handsome priest who eventually becomes a Cardinal of the Roman Catholic Church . . . ." (Don't give away too much of the plot at this time.)

3. Tell about your background. Cite your published credits. If you've written other books, list them by title, publisher, and year of publication. Since you're submitting a fiction work, cite your fiction credits first; then cite your nonfiction credits, if you have any. Cite short stories you may have written, listing publications and publication dates.

What about mentioning any writing or workshop courses you may have taken, or submitting writing samples at the query stage?

Some authorities say it's not important or even advisable to mention a workshop background, or to enclose writing samples. But that may be a matter of opinion. New writers may feel more confident if they can cite some type of writing experience—even if it's just a workshop. And a writer who is trying to sell his or her first book may find submitting short story samples helpful when trying to find an agent to represent him or her. (The query letter you might send to an editor could easily be adapted to send to an agent when seeking one to represent you. See the sample on page 156.)

How long should your query letter be? The shorter, the better, is the best guide to the length of a query letter. But when a writer is unknown to the editor or has no real publishing track record, then the right length for the query letter would be: as long as it needs to be to get enough of the idea across to stimulate the editor's curiosity and get him or her to ask to see your proposal. *But keep in mind that it shouldn't run more than one to one-and-a-half pages.*

Submit your letter on your letterhead stationery; if you don't have any, consider having some made up. Since much of what we do depends on appearance, you'd probably agree that printed letterhead does look more professional than the typewritten variety.

However, you can create your own letterhead: Start approximately one inch from the top of the sheet. Center the following: Top line, your name; next line, your address, including apartment number if relevant; next line, city, state, and zip code; fourth line, area code and telephone number. If you're using a typewriter, go over these lines several times to get the blackest, boldest effect possible; with a computer, consult your software manual for information on how to instruct your printer to boldface the letterhead or set it in a distinctive style of type.

Use the following query letter sample as a general guide in preparing one of your own.

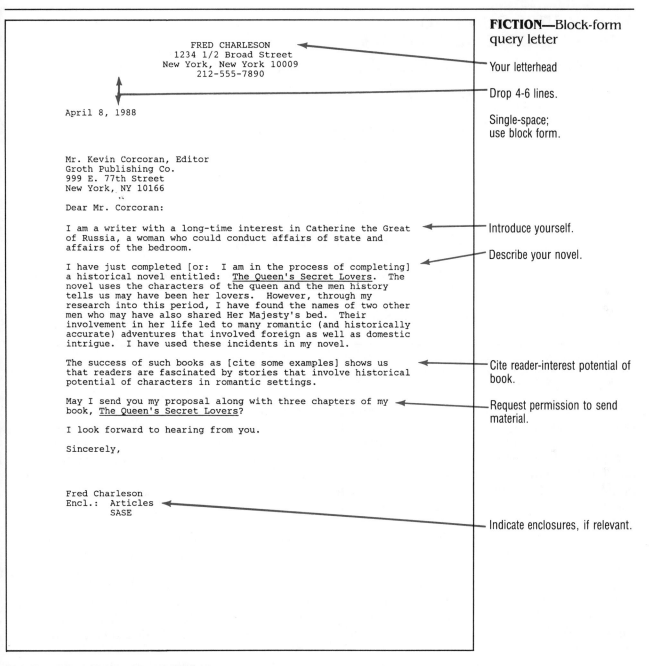

FRED CHARLESON
1234 1/2 Broad Street
New York, New York 10009
212-555-7890

— **FICTION**—Block-form query letter

— Your letterhead

— Drop 4-6 lines.

Single-space; use block form.

April 8, 1988

Mr. Kevin Corcoran, Editor
Groth Publishing Co.
999 E. 77th Street
New York, NY 10166

Dear Mr. Corcoran:

I am a writer with a long-time interest in Catherine the Great of Russia, a woman who could conduct affairs of state and affairs of the bedroom.

— Introduce yourself.

I have just completed [or: I am in the process of completing] a historical novel entitled: <u>The Queen's Secret Lovers</u>. The novel uses the characters of the queen and the men history tells us may have been her lovers. However, through my research into this period, I have found the names of two other men who may have also shared Her Majesty's bed. Their involvement in her life led to many romantic (and historically accurate) adventures that involved foreign as well as domestic intrigue. I have used these incidents in my novel.

— Describe your novel.

The success of such books as [cite some examples] shows us that readers are fascinated by stories that involve historical potential of characters in romantic settings.

— Cite reader-interest potential of book.

May I send you my proposal along with three chapters of my book, <u>The Queen's Secret Lovers</u>?

— Request permission to send material.

I look forward to hearing from you.

Sincerely,

Fred Charleson
Encl.: Articles
       SASE

— Indicate enclosures, if relevant.

V.I.P.—Very Important Point

Make sure you keep a copy of the letter, and make sure you enter it in a Query Letter Submission Log, similar to the Nonfiction Submission Log for Books on page 188. Keep in mind that you're sharing an idea for a work with this letter. You want to be sure you know who saw it, when it was seen, and either when it was answered positively (usually with a request for a more detailed proposal that includes at least three sequential chapters, or for the manuscript itself) or negatively.

AT-A-GLANCE GUIDE TO SUBMITTING FICTION (BOOKS)

The following is a series of steps that many writers follow when submitting their novels:

Prepare the proposal.

Prepare at least three sequential chapters.

Prepare a synopsis of each remaining chapter not included with the proposal.

Prepare the cover letter.

Prepare the package for proper mailing.

Prepare a stamped, self-addressed self mailer for the return of manuscript to you.

Log the submission.

THE NOVEL PROPOSAL: INTRODUCTION

We have a hypothetical author named I. Wright, who has written a hypothetical mystery novel that we're calling *The Rueful Murders in the Morgue.*

We'll show you how I. Wright prepared his proposal and the cover letter that accompanied the proposal when it was sent out—unsolicited—to an editor. (For a sample of a query letter requesting permission to send a proposal, see page 55.)

First, let's start with one of the most frequently asked questions: *Is an outline the same as a proposal?*

The answer is yes and no. An outline can sell a book. Often, all that's needed to include with a detailed outline is a cover letter and the three sample chapters editors usually request. However, in most cases, outlines function as the fleshed-out parts of the proposals, which are, essentially, the skeletal structure on which the book is built. Outlines also exist independently of proposals, functioning as writers' outlines.

Many writers like to work with well-detailed outlines. Others do very well with a looser structure. In any event, the characters in a novel sometimes take on a life of their own as they move through the various plots and subplots. The author then has to deviate from the outline to accommodate these changes (if the changes enhance the book, that is).

What do editors want? Ideally, they'd like to see the entire manuscript of a novel. But realistically, that isn't always possible, nor do they always have the time to go through a novel before making a decision. Therefore, they have to rely on outlines that are presented with enough detail to give them a good idea of the basic structures and flow of the book.

Another question authors sometimes ask: *Is an outline the same as a synopsis?*

Here, too, the answer is a definite—sometimes. An outline should really be a structural detailing of plot and movement. However, in some instances, a briefer synopsis is accepted.

If you think of the outline as the fleshed-out parts of the proposal, you can think of the synopsis as the skin: it conceals the deeper structures from which it draws both its shape and its sustenance, but manages, meanwhile, to present a good idea of what the "body" is all about.

Preparing the Novel Proposal

Think of your proposal as a three-part plan designed to make it easier for you to sell your novel.

Part 1—*The Introduction.* Included here is a basic overview of the book's makeup, for example: how many pages (or words) the manuscript will contain; how close to completion it is.

Generally, an overview of a novel (see page 60) is nowhere as detailed as the overview found in nonfiction proposals (see pages 18, 19). Actually, some authors skip the overview portion of the proposal entirely and rely on a cover letter much like the one on page 65 that accompanies an unsolicited proposal submission.

"About the Author"—the bio that accompanies a proposal—is also found in the Introduction.

Part 2—*The Chapter-by-Chapter Outline.* Each chapter begins on a separate page and the outline—or synopsis—for each chapter can run anywhere from three pages to ten (or, on occasion, more if necessary).

Since you are writing to show the editor not only what your book is all about but also how well you can tell a story, it's important that you make your outline, or synopsis, as lively and interesting as possible. The well-known agent Richard Curtis describes the synopsis as a series of short stories with a beginning, a middle, and an end, written in an engaging style that catches, and keeps, the reader's interest.

One major difference between an outline and a synopsis is the detail content: an outline tends to contain more details surrounding the story, as well as the story itself, while a synopsis tends to concentrate on the story.

For example: A passage from an outline of our hypothetical book, *The Rueful Murders in the Morgue,* might read something like this:

The police detective notices how the blood ran down the window sill into a crevice where he found the woman's glove. The pattern of the blood was a clue to how the killing was committed . . . .

A synopsis might read something like this:

Blood spatters are clues to the way the killer worked. A victim's glove found in a strange place is another clue. . . .

Part 3—*Sample Chapters.* For a novel, you need to submit three chapters. These must be sequential; that is, one must lead into the other. Unlike a nonfiction book, of which chapters are submitted to show diversity in the book's content, a novel needs to present a sense of movement and plot in a well-defined, logical flow. While you can choose any of the three chapters you prefer, it's a good idea to start with Chapter One and move forward. After all, it's not just the ending that makes a mystery work, or a romance sing, or a science fiction tale send your imagination soaring; it's also the way the story is told right from the beginning.

A table of contents is also included in a proposal. This lists the *contents of the proposal,* not of the book. A separate table of contents accompanies the book's manuscript.

On the following pages, I. Wright's proposal for *The Rueful Murders in the Morgue* will begin. Sample pages, diagrammed to indicate margins and space placements, are provided.

Our hypothetical book has five chapters, the first two of which are being attached to the proposal. The outline for each of the chapters follows.

**PROPOSAL SAMPLE
(NOVEL)**—Cover or title
sheet

1-1½″ from top;
single-space.

Center,
halfway down page.

Drop 2 lines;
center.

Drop 2 lines;
center (subtitle).

Drop 4 lines; center.

(If you have an agent, use his
or her name, not yours: put
agent's name and address at
right, with last line 1½″ from
bottom of page.)

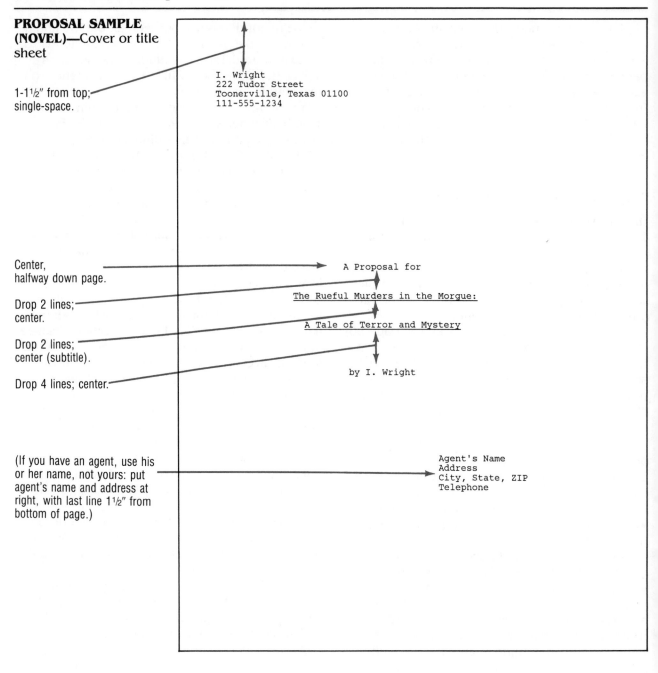

```
         I. Wright
         222 Tudor Street
         Toonerville, Texas 01100
         111-555-1234
```

```
                              A Proposal for

                    The Rueful Murders in the Morgue:

                     A Tale of Terror and Mystery

                             by I. Wright
```

```
                                         Agent's Name
                                         Address
                                         City, State, ZIP
                                         Telephone
```

PROPOSAL SAMPLE (NOVEL)—Table of Contents

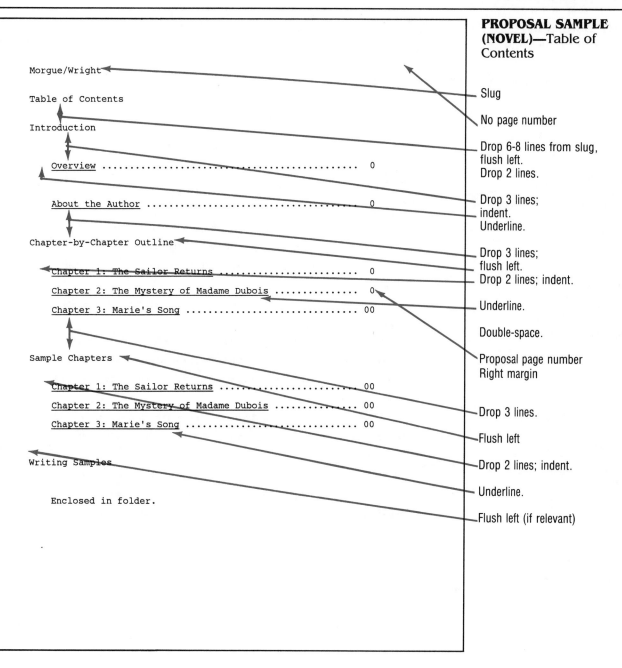

Morgue/Wright

Table of Contents

Introduction

    <u>Overview</u> 0

    <u>About the Author</u> 0

Chapter-by-Chapter Outline

    <u>Chapter 1: The Sailor Returns</u> 0

    <u>Chapter 2: The Mystery of Madame Dubois</u> 0

    <u>Chapter 3: Marie's Song</u> 00

Sample Chapters

    <u>Chapter 1: The Sailor Returns</u> 00

    <u>Chapter 2: The Mystery of Madame Dubois</u> 00

    <u>Chapter 3: Marie's Song</u> 00

Writing Samples

    Enclosed in folder.

Slug

No page number

Drop 6-8 lines from slug, flush left.
Drop 2 lines.

Drop 3 lines; indent.
Underline.

Drop 3 lines; flush left.
Drop 2 lines; indent.

Underline.

Double-space.

Proposal page number
Right margin

Drop 3 lines.

Flush left

Drop 2 lines; indent.

Underline.

Flush left (if relevant)

**PROPOSAL SAMPLE
(NOVEL)**—First page

Slug and page number

Drop 4-6 lines.

Drop 4-6 lines; underline.

Drop 4 lines; indent.
Double-space "grabber" opener.

Cite readership potential.

Give short description of novel.

Cite novel's potential.

Indicate author's promotional activities, if relevant.

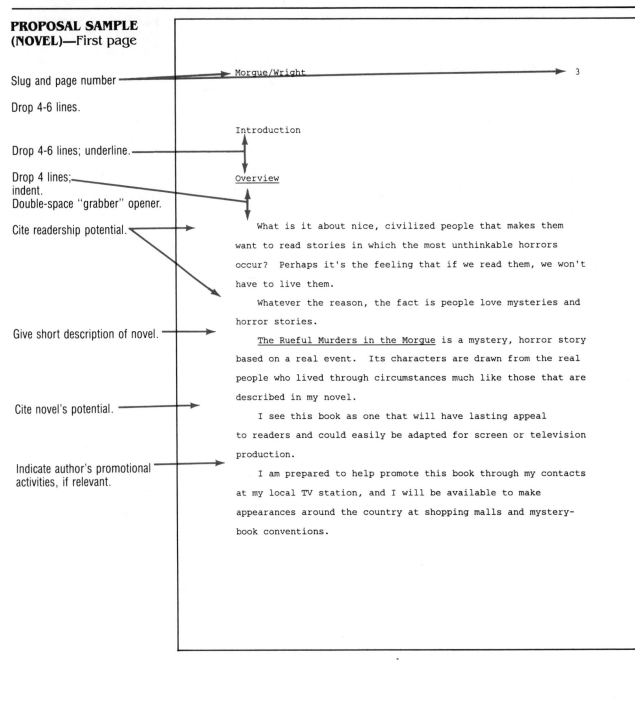

Morgue/Wright   3

Introduction

Overview

    What is it about nice, civilized people that makes them
want to read stories in which the most unthinkable horrors
occur? Perhaps it's the feeling that if we read them, we won't
have to live them.

    Whatever the reason, the fact is people love mysteries and
horror stories.

    The Rueful Murders in the Morgue is a mystery, horror story
based on a real event. Its characters are drawn from the real
people who lived through circumstances much like those that are
described in my novel.

    I see this book as one that will have lasting appeal
to readers and could easily be adapted for screen or television
production.

    I am prepared to help promote this book through my contacts
at my local TV station, and I will be available to make
appearances around the country at shopping malls and mystery-
book conventions.

**PROPOSAL SAMPLE
(NOVEL)**

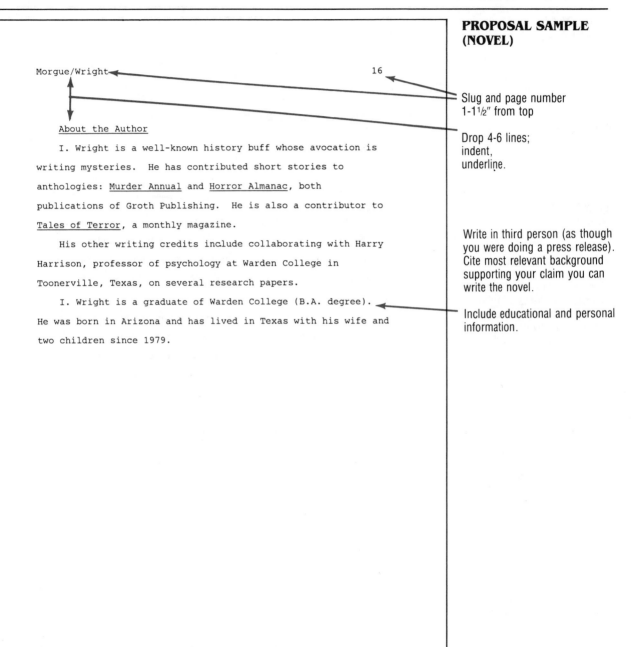

Morgue/Wright   16

About the Author

I. Wright is a well-known history buff whose avocation is
writing mysteries. He has contributed short stories to
anthologies: Murder Annual and Horror Almanac, both
publications of Groth Publishing. He is also a contributor to
Tales of Terror, a monthly magazine.

His other writing credits include collaborating with Harry
Harrison, professor of psychology at Warden College in
Toonerville, Texas, on several research papers.

I. Wright is a graduate of Warden College (B.A. degree).
He was born in Arizona and has lived in Texas with his wife and
two children since 1979.

Slug and page number
1-1½″ from top

Drop 4-6 lines;
indent,
underline.

Write in third person (as though
you were doing a press release).
Cite most relevant background
supporting your claim you can
write the novel.

Include educational and personal
information.

**PROPOSAL
SAMPLE**—Outline

Slug and page number
1-1½" from top.

Drop 4 lines;
underline.

Drop 2 lines.
Chapter name
Number of pages

Drop 2 lines;
indent and double-space.

(Continue with a few sentences
describing each event in this
chapter. Each chapter outline
begins on a new page unless
the material is very short.)

Morgue/Wright   21

Chapter-by-Chapter Outline

Chapter 1

The Sailor Returns   8 pages

This chapter begins with Jean LeBeau returning to Paris in
an attempt to reclaim the wife he lost to his friend, Pierre
Darnel. LeBeau has brought with him from Tahiti a creature
that he has smuggled in from the ship that lies at anchor in
LeHavre.

LeBeau's reception by his estranged wife, Suzanne, is a
cruel one. He slinks away determined to be avenged.

He then goes to the rooming house where his former
shipmate, Yves St. Riviere, had lived before signing on for the
Tahiti run that proved fatal to him.

PROPOSAL SAMPLE—Succeeding chapter

Morgue/Wright   30

Chapter 2

    The Mystery of Madame Dubois   12 pages

    LeBeau allowed himself to have his palm read by the
mysterious woman in the room next to his. He felt a cold chill
when she took his hand. He felt his heart turning into ice as
she stroked his fingers. All the joy he should have felt at
the touch of a woman had turned to fear.

    Madame Dubois had important things to do when LeBeau left,
shaken by what she had told him. She threw off her veil and
left by another exit.

Slug and page number
1-1½" lines from top

Drop 4 lines.

Drop 2 lines;
indent,
double-space.

Without Waiting for an Invitation . . . How to Prepare a Cover Letter to go with an Unsolicited Proposal

Maybe, in most instances, it's a bit pushy to go where you haven't been invited, but sometimes sending a proposal to an editor before being asked to do so can be time-saving for both of you.

As we said several times in this section, it's your manuscript that sells the book; everything else is a sales aid, including the cover letter sent out with an unsolicited proposal. In a sense, it functions as a sort of "pitch letter" that you sometimes see accompanying a sample magazine or sample newsletter a publisher would like you to subscribe to. It helps to call the editor's attention to this unexpected package that's arrived on his or her desk. And, because it has to compete for the editor's time and attention, just like a pitch letter, it should open with one of our *grabbers*. (Sample coming up.)

As we discussed earlier in this section, the question about querying or not querying editors is still a matter of debate among many novelists.

I. Wright has chosen not to send a pre-proposal query.

After researching in *Writer's Market* and *Fiction Writer's Market,* he has determined that the publisher he has chosen to submit to doesn't require one. Instead he's written a comprehensive cover letter to accompany an unsolicited proposal, a sample of which follows. (For guidance in preparing a pre-proposal query, see pages 53-54.)

Some of the basic elements I. Wright chose to put into his cover letter include:

- The opening grabber statement
- Description of the audience he plans to reach
- His qualifications for writing this type of book
- The estimated length of the book
- The estimated time for completion of the book
- Indication that an SASE is enclosed (self-addressed, stamped envelope—manuscript size)

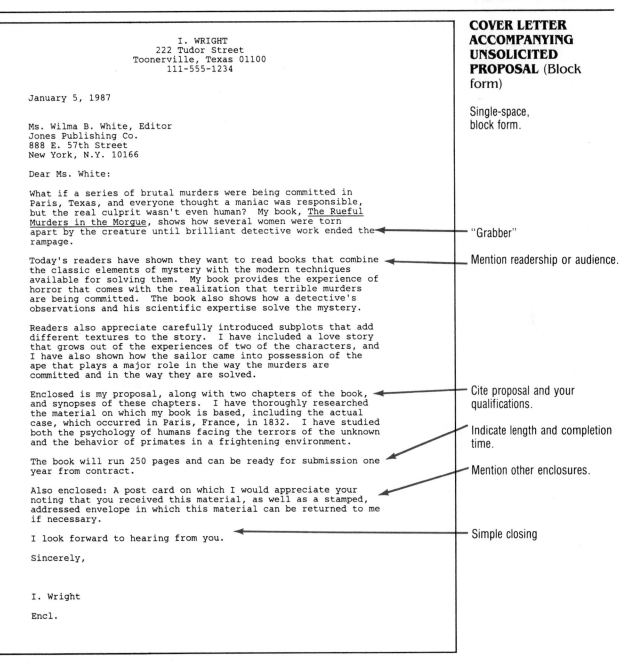

I. WRIGHT
222 Tudor Street
Toonerville, Texas 01100
111-555-1234

January 5, 1987

Ms. Wilma B. White, Editor
Jones Publishing Co.
888 E. 57th Street
New York, N.Y. 10166

Dear Ms. White:

What if a series of brutal murders were being committed in Paris, Texas, and everyone thought a maniac was responsible, but the real culprit wasn't even human? My book, <u>The Rueful Murders in the Morgue</u>, shows how several women were torn apart by the creature until brilliant detective work ended the rampage.

Today's readers have shown they want to read books that combine the classic elements of mystery with the modern techniques available for solving them. My book provides the experience of horror that comes with the realization that terrible murders are being committed. The book also shows how a detective's observations and his scientific expertise solve the mystery.

Readers also appreciate carefully introduced subplots that add different textures to the story. I have included a love story that grows out of the experiences of two of the characters, and I have also shown how the sailor came into possession of the ape that plays a major role in the way the murders are committed and in the way they are solved.

Enclosed is my proposal, along with two chapters of the book, and synopses of these chapters. I have thoroughly researched the material on which my book is based, including the actual case, which occurred in Paris, France, in 1832. I have studied both the psychology of humans facing the terrors of the unknown and the behavior of primates in a frightening environment.

The book will run 250 pages and can be ready for submission one year from contract.

Also enclosed: A post card on which I would appreciate your noting that you received this material, as well as a stamped, addressed envelope in which this material can be returned to me if necessary.

I look forward to hearing from you.

Sincerely,

I. Wright

Encl.

COVER LETTER ACCOMPANYING UNSOLICITED PROPOSAL (Block form)

Single-space, block form.

— "Grabber"

— Mention readership or audience.

— Cite proposal and your qualifications.

— Indicate length and completion time.

— Mention other enclosures.

— Simple closing

AT-A-GLANCE GUIDE TO TYPING
MANUSCRIPT PAGES—FICTION

Margins	Leave 1-1½ inches around text
Title page	No page number.
All manuscript pages	Six lines from top, start at left margin. Type slug: book title in caps, then page number.
Sample	**RUEFUL MURDERS IN THE MORGUE—126**
First page of each new chapter	Drop down 12 lines from top, center or flush left in caps
Sample	**Chapter 1—THE SAILOR RETURNS** Drop 6-8 lines; indent first line of text.
Subsequent pages of each chapter	Drop 6 lines from name slug and page number and start text.
Paper	Good quality (20-pound bond). Computer paper should be laser cut so that when you separate the pages, they will have clean edges.

PAGES—FROM FIRST TO LAST

Every book begins on a first page. That first page is *not* the cover or title sheet. Therefore, when you number the pages of your manuscript, the title sheet remains unpaginated.

These samples follow:

1. A title or cover sheet
2. The first page of a manuscript
3. The second page of a manuscript
4. The first page of a new chapter

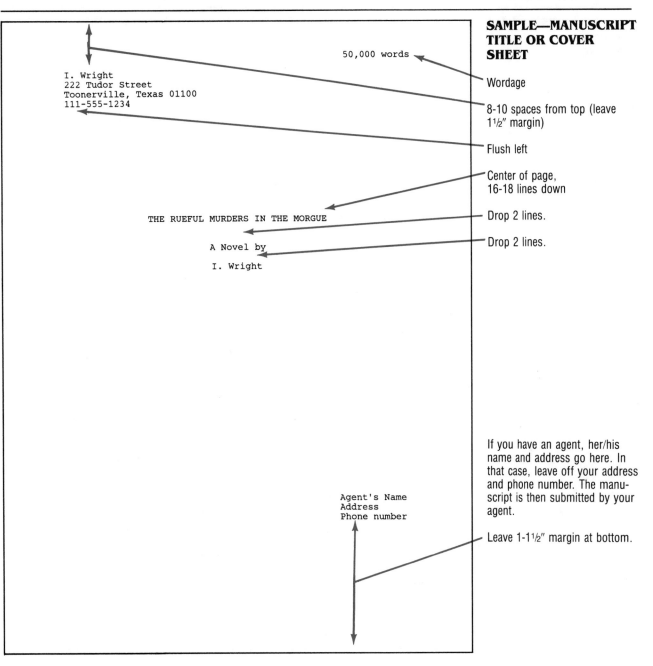

SAMPLE—MANUSCRIPT TITLE OR COVER SHEET

Wordage

8-10 spaces from top (leave 1½″ margin)

Flush left

Center of page, 16-18 lines down

Drop 2 lines.

Drop 2 lines.

If you have an agent, her/his name and address go here. In that case, leave off your address and phone number. The manuscript is then submitted by your agent.

Leave 1-1½″ margin at bottom.

50,000 words

I. Wright
222 Tudor Street
Toonerville, Texas 01100
111-555-1234

THE RUEFUL MURDERS IN THE MORGUE

A Novel by

I. Wright

Agent's Name
Address
Phone number

**SAMPLE—FIRST PAGE
OF NOVEL
MANUSCRIPT**

Drop 1-1½" from top;
type novel's title.

Drop one-third of the way down
from the top of the page.
Title in caps
Center.

Drop 6-8 lines;
Double-space,
indent for text.

End page 1-1½" from bottom

RUEFUL MURDERS IN THE MORGUE   5

CHAPTER 1--THE SAILOR RETURNS

          LeBeau bristled at the thought of what he might find when he

     returned to Paris. He was especially fearful that his terrible

     secret might be discovered.

          He had expected to walk along wet streets. But the weather had

     turned suddenly bright after a morning of rain and fog.

     Surprisingly, LeBeau found the sun disturbing. The darkness in his

     heart seemed easier to carry if the day were also dark. There was

     also a strange feeling that if the sun were bright enough, it would

     betray his secret. "What was it I used to hear as a boy," he

     thought, "that the more a thing needs to be kept hidden, the more

     it betrays its own presence?"

          He sighed, "I want to go back," he said to himself. "But I

     feel this warning, perhaps, that it would be wiser to forget Paris

     and to flee."

          He smiled a thin, cruel smile. "But I don't really want to go

RUEFUL MURDERS IN THE MORGUE--Chapter 2   50

    The policeman seemed to come out of nowhere. LeBeau panicked.
His throat tightened. He licked the sweat on his upper lip. His
legs felt weak. He caught himself: "If I don't watch it, I'll
betray myself," he thought.

    He recalled a shipmate talking about being aboard a vessel
that hauled in survivors from the sunken Grande Quenelles. One of
the survivors had killed another one for his water ration during
one of their nights adrift in the lifeboat. No one knew who the
killer was.

    "But I had my suspicions," his shipmate said. "There was one
who always looked around to see where the other men were before he
settled down. He always tried to stay closer to one of us. He
must have felt that they knew who the killer was all along and were
planning to kill him when no one from our crew could see them."

    LeBeau straighted his shoulders. He would act as if there
were no reason to be startled by the sight of a policeman, or
anyone else.

    The policeman seemed to come out of nowhere. LeBeau panicked.
His throat tightened. He licked the sweat on his upper lip. His
legs felt weak. He caught himself: "If I don't watch it, I'll
betray myself," he thought.

    He recalled a shipmate talking about being aboard a vessel
that hauled in survivors from the sunken Grande Quenelles. One

---

SAMPLE—Second page of novel manuscript OR Second page of any new chapter

Start 1-1½" from top; slug of novel's title, chapter number and manuscript page number.

Double-space.

End page 1-1½" from bottom.

SAMPLE MANUSCRIPT PAGE—Showing first page of new chapter

Drop 1-1½″ from top. Type novel name.

Drop 4-6 lines; type chapter name and number. Can be centered or flush left

Drop 6-8 lines; indent. Double-space.

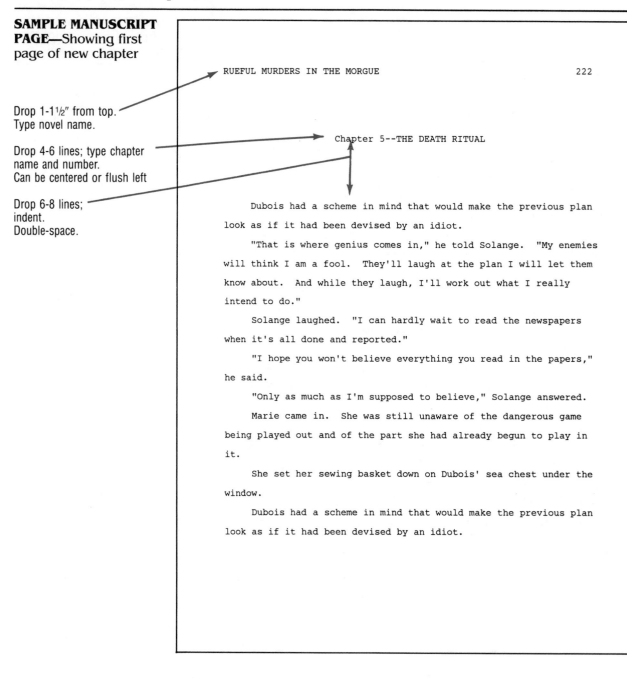

RUEFUL MURDERS IN THE MORGUE   222

                        Chapter 5--THE DEATH RITUAL

        Dubois had a scheme in mind that would make the previous plan

    look as if it had been devised by an idiot.

        "That is where genius comes in," he told Solange. "My enemies

    will think I am a fool. They'll laugh at the plan I will let them

    know about. And while they laugh, I'll work out what I really

    intend to do."

        Solange laughed. "I can hardly wait to read the newspapers

    when it's all done and reported."

        "I hope you won't believe everything you read in the papers,"

    he said.

        "Only as much as I'm supposed to believe," Solange answered.

        Marie came in. She was still unaware of the dangerous game

    being played out and of the part she had already begun to play in

    it.

        She set her sewing basket down on Dubois' sea chest under the

    window.

        Dubois had a scheme in mind that would make the previous plan

    look as if it had been devised by an idiot.

AT-A-GLANCE GUIDE TO FRONT MATTER IN NOVELS

Contents   Required. Type on separate page—do not number.

Dedication   Optional. Type on separate page—do not number.

Epigraph

The epigraph (or *inscription* when used as front matter) is a short quotation that has relevance to the contents of the book, and it is optional. Source must always be given. When used at the beginning of a chapter, an epigraph is a quotation that pertains to the contents of the chapter.

In a book   Type on separate page—do not number.

At chapter heading   Type on the same page on which the chapter begins. Source must always be given.

Foreword   Optional. Type on a separate page—do not number. A foreword is usually written by another author in the same genre.

Preface

This is optional, and used if the author wants to explain why he or she wrote the book. The preface is also used to acknowledge the people and/or institutions that were of help in preparing the book. This is always written by the author, who signs it with his or her initials and indicates the place where and the date the preface was written. (*Note:* Your editor will determine if the publisher's style uses place and date as well as author's name or initials. You are advised to type them in nonetheless.) Type the preface on a separate page—do not number.

Acknowledgments

Again, this is optional, and is used if there are more people and/or institutions than can be acknowledged in the preface. As with the preface, the author signs with his or her initials and the place and date the acknowledgments were written. (The same note as given under preface applies here.) Type acknowledgments on a separate page—do not number.

SAMPLE COVER LETTER WITH MANUSCRIPT

Margins: 1-1½″ all around

Letterhead

Date

Drop 4 lines;
Use block form.

Double-space between short paragraphs.

Simple closing

Enclosures

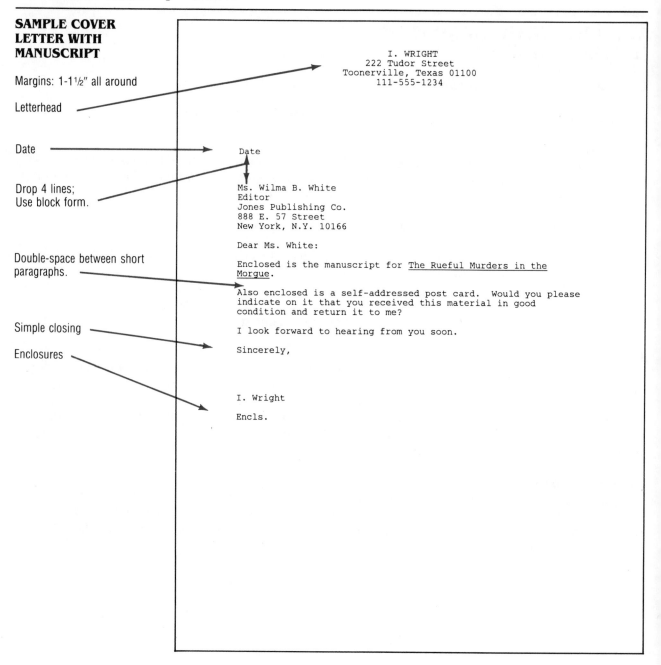

```
                         I. WRIGHT
                      222 Tudor Street
                   Toonerville, Texas 01100
                      111-555-1234




     Date


     Ms. Wilma B. White
     Editor
     Jones Publishing Co.
     888 E. 57 Street
     New York, N.Y. 10166

     Dear Ms. White:

     Enclosed is the manuscript for The Rueful Murders in the
     Morgue.

     Also enclosed is a self-addressed post card.  Would you please
     indicate on it that you received this material in good
     condition and return it to me?

     I look forward to hearing from you soon.

     Sincerely,



     I. Wright

     Encls.
```

LETTER INQUIRING ON STATUS OF MANUSCRIPT

```
                    I. WRIGHT
                 222 Tudor Street
               Toonerville, Texas 01100
                   111-555-1234
```

— Letterhead

```
Date




Ms. Wilma B. White
Editor
Jones Publishing Co.
888 E. 57 Street
New York, N.Y. 10166

Dear Ms. White:

On December 23, 1987 I sent you my manuscript, Rueful Murders
in the Morgue.  You sent back my self-addressed reply card
indicating that it had been received by you in good condition
on December 29.

It has been three months since the manuscript was delivered,
and I would appreciate your letting me know what its status is
at this time.

I have enclosed a self-addressed, stamped envelope for your
convenience in replying.

Thank you.

Sincerely,



I. Wright
```

— Information according to your records

— In accordance with this company's usual practice

— Enclose self-addressed stamped envelope

— Simple closing

FOLLOWING UP

It's perfectly natural to wonder what's become of your manuscript once it's reached the publishing house. Response time varies from publisher to publisher, so it is wise to check the listings in *Fiction Writer's Market* or the guidelines for contributors provided by the company. However, if that time has passed by several weeks and you haven't heard a word, most editors will understand if you make an inquiry. You may want to send a letter something like the one on this page.

PART 2

Short Forms

Short Forms is an editorial term that takes in just about every type of written material that is not, technically, a book or a script. The types of writing most often considered short forms are magazine articles (nonfiction), short stories, fillers, poems, greeting cards, anecdotes, and recipes.

In this section, we'll discuss these short forms in general, and we'll provide samples and explanations of various types of fillers. In addition, you'll learn how to prepare manuscript pages, cover letters, queries, and release forms for photographers; how to reckon word counts for short story manuscripts; and how to submit short forms for publication.

Sample pages will be provided and diagrammed to show appropriate margin widths and line spacing, as well as placement of elements on a page. This section also provides valuable guides that will help you through each step.

In short, by the time you finish this section on short forms, you'll be able to deal with all of your work on a professional level—and be able to submit a manuscript or a filler that looks good enough to read.

MAGAZINE ARTICLES

This section should answer just about any question you've ever had about manuscript preparation for nonfiction magazine articles.

True, we can't tell you which editors are easier to sell than others, but we can show you how to present a manuscript that indicates to an editor that you are a professional who takes the time to do things right.

We'll also show you how to write query letters that could lead to an assignment.

You'll see samples of manuscript pages, a title page (not always required), a query letter, a cover letter, and follow-up letters.

Query or Proposal?

We have used the word *proposal* many times in this book. However, the usual practice with nonfiction articles is to begin with a query letter to an editor which can function as a proposal, as you'll see in the following sample.

There are several good reasons why a query letter is a good idea:

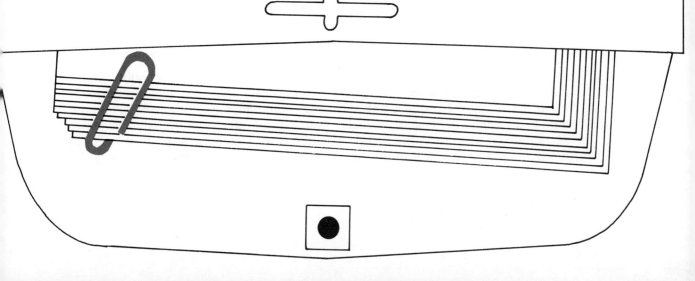

SAMPLE QUERY LETTER—Magazine— nonfiction (Block form)

Margins: 1-1½″ all around

Letterhead

Date

Date

Addressee

Introduce yourself and cite writing background or expertise.

Talk about article's background and development.

Cite photos if relevant.

Tell why magazine would want article and request permission to send.

Closing

```
                                    BONNIE GREY
                                  1234 56 Drive
                             Brooklyn, New York 11250
                              Telephone 718-555-1987


        Date


        Mr. Donald Duncan, Editor
        Fashion Plus Magazine
        999 West 99th Street
        New York, New York 10055

        Dear Mr. Duncan:

        I am a freelance writer specializing in handicrafts and
        fashion.  My work has appeared in several publications
        including Charming Woman, Blue Grass Monthly, and Vermont
        Antiques Journal.

        I recently attended a handicrafts festival in Knoxville,
        Tennessee, and was very much impressed by the way the designers
        were able to combine current fashion elements with traditional
        "mountain" dress.  I interviewed several people, including the
        designers, the historians, and the weavers who provided the
        traditional cloth used for the designs.

        I was also able to take pictures of the event, and I'm
        enclosing two black-and-white blowups from one of the rolls I
        used.  I also took several rolls of color.

        I feel that my article, "Tennessee's Fashion Future Comes Out
        of Its Past," is very much in keeping with Fashion Plus
        editorial policies.  May I send it to you, along with several
        transparencies and a b&w contact sheet?

        I look forward to hearing from you.

        Sincerely,


        BONNIE GREY

        Encls.
```

1. The flood of unsolicited manuscripts into a magazine editor's office does not provide a welcoming climate for an unexpected new arrival.

2. Editors tend to assign on the basis of actual need: a query letter gets read long before an unsolicited manuscript is even opened. If what you suggest tallies with what the publication needs, you have a chance to sell your proposed article.

3. Sometimes the idea proposed in the query letter is not quite what the editor is looking for but sparks a variation that the writer of the query letter is requested to do.

Manuscript—Magazine Article

In most cases, you will not need to use a title page when you submit a manuscript for a magazine article.

The information usually found on a title sheet (see page 80) can be transferred to the first page of your manuscript (see sample, page 81). Consult the following At-a-Glance Guide for correct format of your magazine article manuscript.

AT-A-GLANCE GUIDE TO
MAGAZINE ARTICLE FORMAT

Manuscript First Page

Indicate	Your name, address, and telephone number
	The rights you're selling with the article (usually First North American Rights, unless the writer has made a different agreement with the editor)
	Word count of article; the approximate number rounded off
	Article's title and (if relevant) subtitle
	Writer's name (If you don't intend to use your own name on the article, indicate your pseudonym below the title.)
Do not indicate	Page number

Subsequent Pages of Article Manuscript

These pages generally include the following:

Slug or header

This is made up of a word or two from the title and the writer's last name. It is important for identification of the article in the event the pages are separated and mixed with other manuscript pages.

Slug placement	Flush left at upper-left corner is the preferred placement.
Page number	Pages are numbered from page 2 on—number is usually placed at upper-right margin.
Margin spacing	Leave 1¼" to 1½" margin around text.
Last page	All of the above, plus indication of manuscript completion. For nonfiction articles, drop 4 lines from end of text and type: *-00-* or *THE END* or *-30-*. (*Note:* -30- is almost always used for newspaper copy and is also popular with magazine writers.)

Spacing and Placement

First page of magazine article

Note: most writers use this page as a title page as well as a text page. Directions are given for this combined-page setup.

Writer's name, address, and phone	Single-space; flush left at upper left margin. Type 1-1½" from top of page.
Rights	Set upper right-hand corner, 1¼" to 1½" below top of page.
Word count	Set below Rights.
Title	Drop 20 lines from top; center, CAPITALIZE.
Writer's name (or pseudonym)	Drop 4 lines from title; center.
Text	Drop 4 lines from writer's name. Double-space; indent first word of each paragraph.
Second (and subsequent) manuscript pages	
Slug or header	Flush left 1¼" to 1½" from top.
Page numbers	Start on page 2; place upper right, 1-1½" from top, on same line with slug or header.
End of manuscript (nonfiction article)	Use symbol such as *** or *-00-* or *-30-*.

BONNIE GREY
1234 56 Drive
Brooklyn, New York 11250
Telephone 718-555-1987

Letterhead

Use block form.

January 2, 1988

Mr. Donald Duncan, Editor
Fashion Plus Magazine
999 West 99th Street
New York, N.Y. 10055

Addressee

Dear Mr. Duncan:

Enclosed is my article, Tennessee's Future Comes Out of Its
Past, which was due on January 10. I'm pleased that I was able
to have it for you ahead of deadline.

Cite name of article and date it
was due; (meeting deadlines is
essential).

I am also enclosing three transparencies from the Tennessee
Tourist Office. These color slides show the pottery shop
(which is discussed in my article) in operation. Also enclosed
is a caption sheet provided by the Tennessee Tourist Office.

Drop 2 lines;
cite other enclosures if relevant.
(See page 175 for data on
mailing photos.)

I enjoyed working on this article, and I look forward to
hearing your comments.

A pleasant exchange is always
welcome.

Sincerely,

Drop 2 lines for closing.

Drop 4 lines.

BONNIE GREY

Enclosures

Drop 2 lines.

SAMPLE TITLE PAGE—Magazine article

Margins: 1-1½" all around

Note rights, indicate wordage.

Place title halfway down page; can be centered, as shown, or flush left.

Drop 2 lines between title and "by;" then 1 line and author. (If you use a pseudonym, indicate it here.)

Address only, flush left. (Add your name only if you've used a pseudonym for the article.)

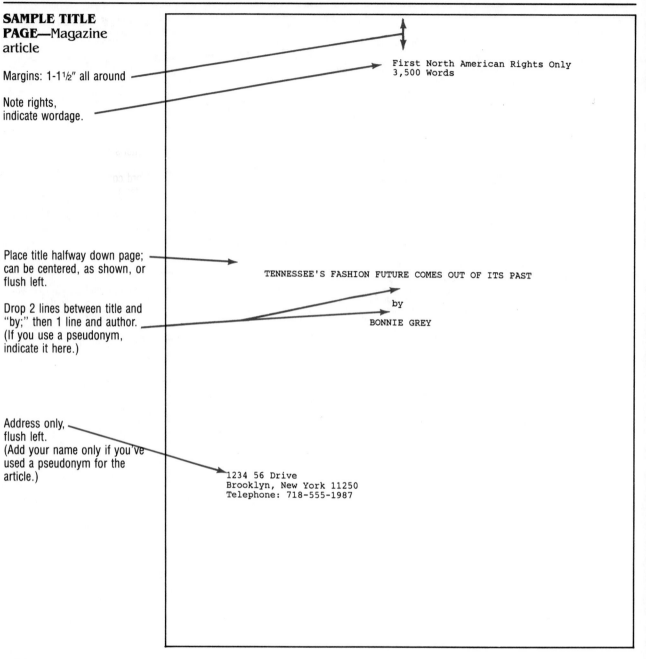

```
                                        First North American Rights Only
                                        3,500 Words




                 TENNESSEE'S FASHION FUTURE COMES OUT OF ITS PAST

                                        by
                                  BONNIE GREY




        1234 56 Drive
        Brooklyn, New York 11250
        Telephone: 718-555-1987
```

Title Page

Most writers do not use a title page for their magazine articles—and most editors don't require one.

However, we've found that when a writer uses a pseudonym on an article, it's helpful to use a title sheet on which the pseudonym is indicated.

The preferred version, which combines title page and manuscript, follows.

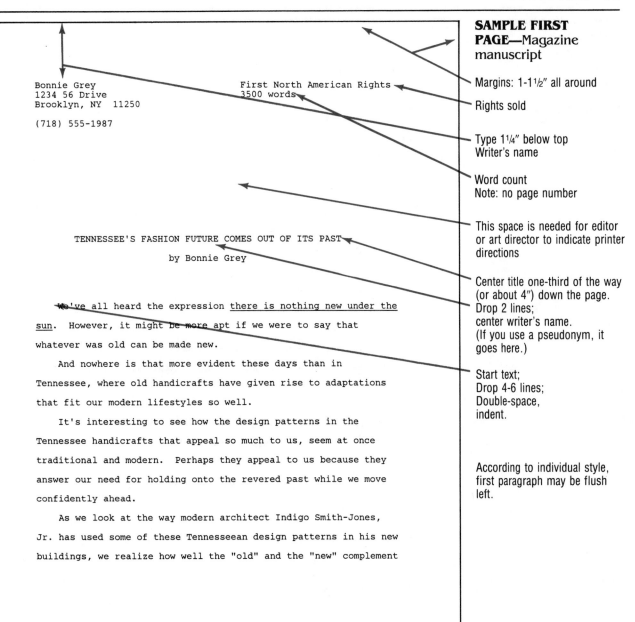

SAMPLE FIRST PAGE—Magazine manuscript

Margins: 1-1½" all around

Rights sold

Type 1¼" below top
Writer's name

Word count
Note: no page number

This space is needed for editor or art director to indicate printer directions

Center title one-third of the way (or about 4") down the page.
Drop 2 lines;
center writer's name.
(If you use a pseudonym, it goes here.)

Start text;
Drop 4-6 lines;
Double-space,
indent.

According to individual style, first paragraph may be flush left.

Bonnie Grey
1234 56 Drive
Brooklyn, NY 11250

(718) 555-1987

First North American Rights
3500 words

TENNESSEE'S FASHION FUTURE COMES OUT OF ITS PAST

by Bonnie Grey

We've all heard the expression <u>there is nothing new under the sun</u>. However, it might be more apt if we were to say that whatever was old can be made new.

And nowhere is that more evident these days than in Tennessee, where old handicrafts have given rise to adaptations that fit our modern lifestyles so well.

It's interesting to see how the design patterns in the Tennessee handicrafts that appeal so much to us, seem at once traditional and modern. Perhaps they appeal to us because they answer our need for holding onto the revered past while we move confidently ahead.

As we look at the way modern architect Indigo Smith-Jones, Jr. has used some of these Tennesseean design patterns in his new buildings, we realize how well the "old" and the "new" complement

SAMPLE SECOND PAGE—And all subsequent pages—Magazine article manuscript

Slug and page number 1-1½" below top of page.

Drop 4-6 lines.

Double-space.

Grey/Tennessee   2

the problem lies not so much in the way the designs are adapted, as in the way the adaptations reflect their origins.

That's where the people of Tennessee have made their valuable contributions.

The first thing they did was to resist plunging headlong into the modern market. It would have been much easier for them to pretend they didn't know the difference between any of their traditional patterns and something that's come out of textile mill's computer. But they didn't do that. They stuck to the designs that make the pattern honest. In this way, they not only preserved the origins of the pattern, they also preserved their sense of heritage.

If virtue is its own reward, all right. But sometimes it can also be rewarded in a more tangible way. Ironically, by resisting the quick buck and by staying honest, the value of the patterns has increased.

The people showed they understood that what they had to sell was uniquely theirs; something to take pride in and something to protect.

That's not to say the modern world hasn't moved in significant ways. The power loom and the hand loom have been used to give of their respective "strengths" to best develop the technology system to be used in bringing the patterns to the outside world.

Leave 1-1½" at bottom.

Grey/Tennessee   12

Slug and page number 1-1½" below top.

Drop 4 lines.

As we move on to the next step in the manufacture of these classically designed materials, we can expect other periods and other cultural influences to be utilized as well.

It's important to remember that what a culture produces is often appreciated differently by outsiders. Sometimes a beautifully crafted wooden "hope" chest is put in the attic when it's not needed because no one thinks of it as anything more than a handy home artifact.

The same may be true for bowls and jars that come off the pottery wheel. They're utensils, the feeling goes: not important handicrafts.

Going back to fabric and design, it should be stressed that often what we "outsiders" view as artistic expression may be seen by the craftspersons as nothing more than traditional designs they like well enough to carry down the generations with them.

The next move is up to the people of Tennessee who may decide that it's all right to share their heritage with others.

-00-

Note: You can also type -30- or THE END.

SAMPLE—Letter
inquiring about status
of non-assigned article

Margins: 1-1½″ all around

Letterhead

Addressee

Cite article name and date sent;
note date of query and date of
editor's request.

Drop 2 lines;
cite time lapse.

Note enclosure of reply post
card and request for update on
manuscript status.

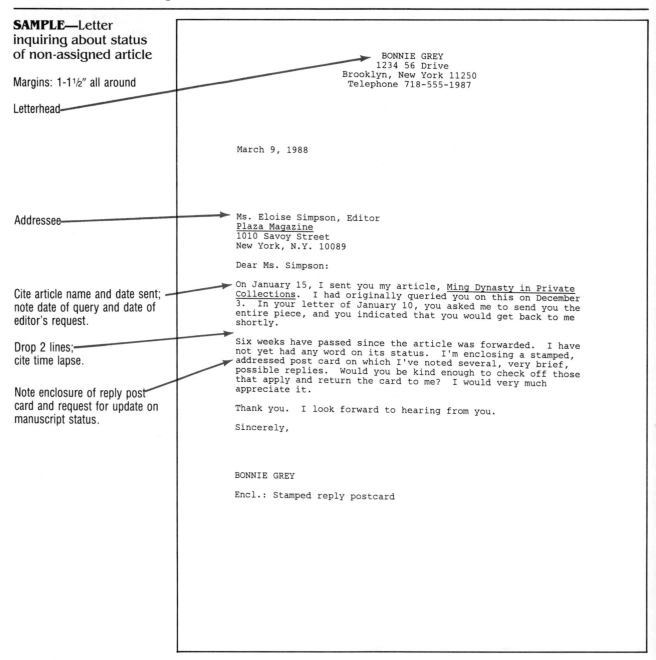

```
                                    BONNIE GREY
                                    1234 56 Drive
                             Brooklyn, New York 11250
                             Telephone 718-555-1987



          March 9, 1988




          Ms. Eloise Simpson, Editor
          Plaza Magazine
          1010 Savoy Street
          New York, N.Y. 10089

          Dear Ms. Simpson:

          On January 15, I sent you my article, Ming Dynasty in Private
          Collections.  I had originally queried you on this on December
          3.  In your letter of January 10, you asked me to send you the
          entire piece, and you indicated that you would get back to me
          shortly.

          Six weeks have passed since the article was forwarded.  I have
          not yet had any word on its status.  I'm enclosing a stamped,
          addressed post card on which I've noted several, very brief,
          possible replies.  Would you be kind enough to check off those
          that apply and return the card to me?  I would very much
          appreciate it.

          Thank you.  I look forward to hearing from you.

          Sincerely,



          BONNIE GREY

          Encl.: Stamped reply postcard
```

Inquiring About Your Manuscript's Status

Manuscripts that are submitted as the result of definite assignments are usually given prompt attention when they arrive at a magazine. However, sometimes an editor simply asks to see on speculation a manuscript that had been suggested in a query letter. That request doesn't obligate the editor to buy the manuscript when it comes in. And although all submissions should properly be handled as quickly as possible, that doesn't always happen.

How long should you wait to inquire after you've sent in an article that was not assigned?

Depending on the type of magazine and the work flow, you may not hear one way or another about your manuscript's acceptance or rejection for two months. Consult *Writer's Market* for information on how soon some publications usually respond to queries and submissions.

At some point, however, you'll want to make an inquiry. The above sample letter and the following sample reply postcard provide helpful guides.

LOVE USA 22

Bonnie Grey
1234 56 Drive
Brooklyn, NY 11250

SAMPLE—Reply postcard to accompany letter inquiring about manuscript status

Front of card

Your name and address

Bonnie Grey, 1234 56 Dr., Brooklyn, NY 11250/ 718-555-1987
Date_____
Yes, your article, (Ming Dynasty in Private Collections)
was received in my office on_____.

No, we never received your article.(check if relevant)[ ]

We are interested and need more time, and will be in
touch with you. [ ]
We are not interested and will return your article. [ ]
We returned your article on_____.

Other comments:

_____   _____
Signature   Company

Back of card

WHO, WHAT, WHERE, WHEN, HOW . . .

General Submission Logs

We're not discussing the important elements of *writing* a story or article at this point. But the interrogative pronouns that make up the title on this page may well be asked by you any number of times throughout your writing career as you struggle to find out who bought—or didn't respond to—your story submission; what comments they made; where you sent it in the first place, or the second, or . . .; when you sent it; when you got a reply; how it was sent.

Using the handy Submission Logs in Et Cetera on pages 190-191 (one for articles and one for short stories) will give you a permanent record of what you did with your manuscript and what others did with it as well.

SHORT STORIES

Short-story writing is a viable and popular medium. Today, such writers as Joyce Carol Oates and Raymond Carver seem to carry on the tradition of such brilliant short story writers as Shirley Jackson, Edgar Allan Poe, O. Henry, and others who could create vivid images in just a few (compared to a book) pages.

Many of the greatest short story writers whose works we read in anthologies were first published in magazines. That's still the primary outlet for today's writers.

On the following pages, you'll find an "At-a-Glance" Guide to typing a short story, samples of short story manuscript pages, and a sample cover letter that might be sent with a manuscript submission.

AT-A-GLANCE GUIDE TO TYPING A SHORT STORY MANUSCRIPT

When you prepare a manuscript for a short story, the same basic rules would apply as for a novel:

Spacing   Double-space copy.

Margins   Leave 1-1½" around text.

Paper   Use good quality (nonerasable) 20-pound stock; no typos and no obvious corrections.

Word Count   The approximate number of words in your manuscript needs to be shown: this can appear either on the title page or, if you're not using a title page, on the first page of your manuscript (see samples). One way to arrive at a word count is to assume the average line of text contains 10 words: multiply that number by the number of lines on the page (usually 25), and then multiply that result by the number of pages in your manuscript. Make adjustments for very short pages or for pages that start further down for new chapters. Round off number to 50 or 100 (e.g., approx. 3,500 words).

Cover Letter   The cover letter that accompanies unsolicited short stories (as is often the case, since most writers do not query on short stories) contains the following information:
1. Title of the short story
2. Approximate word count
3. Indication of SASE enclosure

Submission Policies

It's a good idea to consult *Fiction Writer's Market (FWM)* for information, such as submission policies, about publications that take short-form fiction. Check the listings in *FWM* carefully before sending out material.

Before sending material, check current editor's name in magazine masthead. Also, check a directory to see if the publication requires a pre-submission query.

Title page (or cover sheet)

Generally, there's no need to prepare a separate title page for a short story. The first page of the manuscript contains the author's name and address; the story's title and, if relevant, subtitle; the author's pseudonym, if relevant; word count; and rights information.

Cover letter

A short story is usually submitted in its entirety with a short cover letter that introduces the theme of the story and provides other important information. The following cover letter sample provides a guide you might want to use when submitting your short story.

SAMPLE—Cover letter accompanying unsolicited short story

Margins: 1-1½″ all around

Letterhead

Use block form; single-space.

Drop 4 lines.

State title of short story. Describe background or theme of story (optional).

Indicate wordage.

Cite professional credits if relevant.

Always enclose this.

Closing

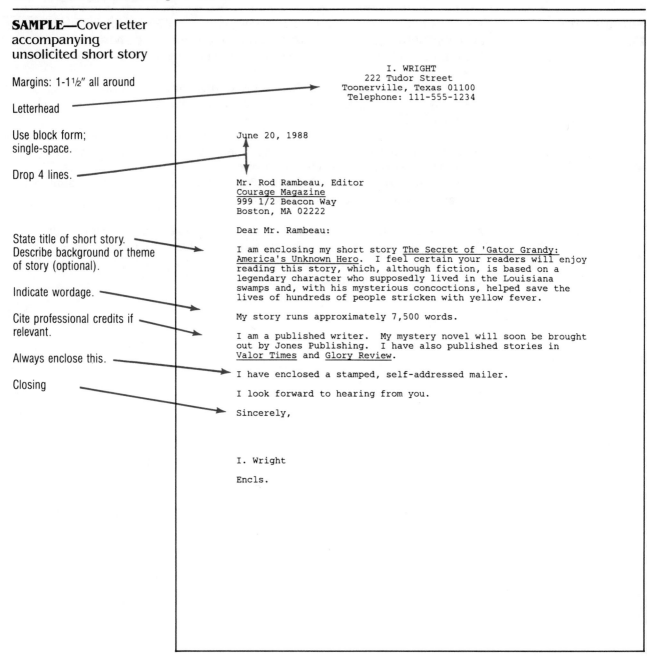

```
                              I. WRIGHT
                           222 Tudor Street
                       Toonerville, Texas 01100
                       Telephone: 111-555-1234


June 20, 1988



Mr. Rod Rambeau, Editor
Courage Magazine
999 1/2 Beacon Way
Boston, MA 02222

Dear Mr. Rambeau:

I am enclosing my short story The Secret of 'Gator Grandy:
America's Unknown Hero.  I feel certain your readers will enjoy
reading this story, which, although fiction, is based on a
legendary character who supposedly lived in the Louisiana
swamps and, with his mysterious concoctions, helped save the
lives of hundreds of people stricken with yellow fever.

My story runs approximately 7,500 words.

I am a published writer.  My mystery novel will soon be brought
out by Jones Publishing.  I have also published stories in
Valor Times and Glory Review.

I have enclosed a stamped, self-addressed mailer.

I look forward to hearing from you.

Sincerely,



I. Wright

Encls.
```

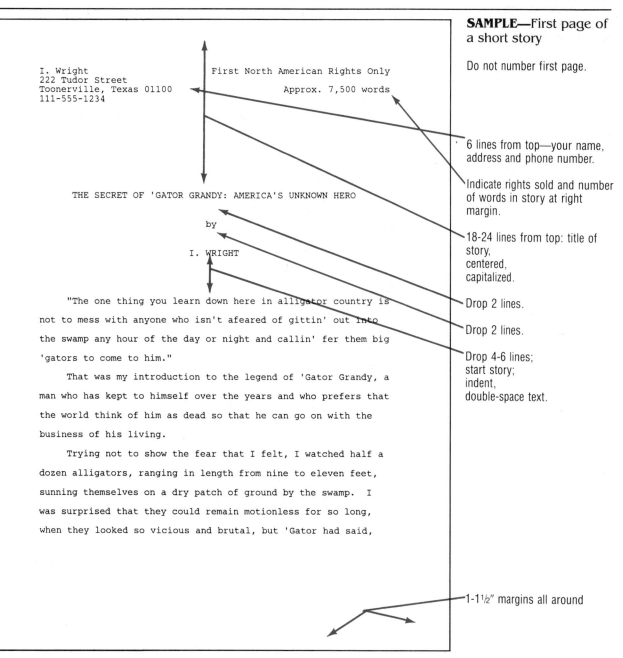

Do not number first page.

I. Wright
222 Tudor Street
Toonerville, Texas 01100
111-555-1234

First North American Rights Only

Approx. 7,500 words

6 lines from top—your name, address and phone number.

Indicate rights sold and number of words in story at right margin.

THE SECRET OF 'GATOR GRANDY: AMERICA'S UNKNOWN HERO

18-24 lines from top: title of story,
centered,
capitalized.

by

Drop 2 lines.

I. WRIGHT

Drop 2 lines.

Drop 4-6 lines;
start story;
indent,
double-space text.

"The one thing you learn down here in alligator country is not to mess with anyone who isn't afeared of gittin' out into the swamp any hour of the day or night and callin' fer them big 'gators to come to him."

That was my introduction to the legend of 'Gator Grandy, a man who has kept to himself over the years and who prefers that the world think of him as dead so that he can go on with the business of his living.

Trying not to show the fear that I felt, I watched half a dozen alligators, ranging in length from nine to eleven feet, sunning themselves on a dry patch of ground by the swamp. I was surprised that they could remain motionless for so long, when they looked so vicious and brutal, but 'Gator had said,

1-1½" margins all around

SAMPLE—Second page
of a short story

Page number

Drop 1-1½″ from top of page.

Author's name

Drop 6-8 lines;
Double-space copy.

Wright   2

It wasn't until after supper that the story about Gator began
coming through. I sat, transfixed, letting my mind take me back
over the years and into that mysterious swamp.

The smells were the first sensations I relived. Some were
sweet, like a thousand hibiscus blossoms opening up all at once.
Some stunk of death: the stench of a carcass, somewhere, that
hadn't become some other creature's meal yet, or hadn't been
absorbed back into the thirsty earth below my feet.

I remembered thinking: it's so wet and dank and yet it seems
perpetually thirsty. The land. It never seems to get enough to
drink.

Now I was hearing about Gator and I wondered: what memories,
what sights, what sounds, would he take away with him if he left
the swamp?

I moved closer and found myself caught up in the Gator
mystique as surely as if I had been there when it all began.

It wasn't until after supper that the story about Gator began
coming through. I sat, transfixed, letting my mind take me back
over the years and into that mysterious swamp.

The smells were the first sensations I relived. Some were
sweet, like a thousand hibiscus blossoms opening up all at once.
Some stunk of death: the stench of a carcass, somewhere, that

End page 1-1½″ from bottom

SAMPLE—Last page of manuscript for short story

Wright   29

Drop 1-1½″ from top of page.

Author's name and page number

Drop 6-8 lines.
Double-space copy.

     Gator knew he couldn't hang around.   He didn't need the
honors. He had done what he had done for the fact that it was
the right thing to do. He remembered Sally always telling him
that you can't turn away from any livin' creature that needed
you.

     But now, it was over. His good deeds were done, and it
was time for him to go back into the swamp, for good.

               THE END

When story is finished,
drop 4 lines;
center,
capitalize.
(Note: THE END is the preferred way to indicate the manuscript is complete.)

POETRY

Sonnets, limericks, odes, epics, haiku—the variety of poetic form is considerable. Whichever you prefer is up to you. However, we can help you type it so that when it's presented to a magazine or anthology editor, its appearance will do you proud.

Remember to use good quality (20-pound bond) paper; *never* use the erasable stuff. Use standard pica or elite type in your typewriter, or similar typefaces, such as courier or letter gothic, for your computer printer. *Never* use the more exotic fonts, such as Olde English or Italic.

Unlike most manuscript submissions for which *the fewer folds, the better* is the preferred form, it's considered all right to send poems folded over twice and put into a regular business-size (#10) envelope. Of course, we're talking about an enclosure of less than twenty pages *plus* a folded SASE (stamped, self-addressed envelope). Refer to *Poet's Market* (Writer's Digest Books) for additional specifications of poetry publishers.

Do you double-space or single-space between lines? Although there is a difference of opinion, our feeling is: When in doubt, double! After all, it's easier to read, and we want to do whatever we can to encourage an editorial reading.

Included in this section is a six-point typing guide that will help you prepare your manuscript, as well as samples of poems with diagrammed instructions to indicate important placements.

Poetry Format

No amount of excellent, clear typing will help to create an exciting or original poem, but keeping to professional standards will enhance your presentation.

Whenever possible, follow these typing suggestions:

1. Type each poem on a separate page.
2. Center the title.
3. In advance of typing, work out suitable *margins*. Poems are not presented with the same margins as essays or stories. Visually, it is best to *center* each poem. Practice on the longest line first and work out equal margins on each side of the page. Center short poems in the middle of the page.
4. Double-space between each line (OR single-space between lines).
5. Triple-space between stanzas (OR double-space between stanzas).
6. When typing an exceptionally long line, single-space and indent runover words five spaces.

Alfred, Lord Tennyson
Somewhere Inn
Countryside, England
(111) 222-3333

                    CROSSING THE BAR

         Sunset and evening star,
         And one clear call for me!
         And may there be no moaning
              of the bar,
         When I put out to sea,

         But such a tide as moving
              seems asleep,
         Too full for sound and foam,
         When that which drew from out
              the boundless deep
         Turns again home.

SAMPLE POEM—
Single-space format

Your name/address/telephone

Center
Capitalize Title

Single-space.
Indent runover lines 5 spaces.

Double-space between stanzas.
Single-space between each line.

SAMPLE POEM—
Double-space format

Your name/address/telephone ⟶

    Elizabeth Barrett Browning
    Barclay Square
    London, England
    (444)555-6666

Center ⟶
Capitalize title

                                        HOW DO I LOVE THEE

                    How do I love thee? Let me count the
                        ways.

Center poem

                    I love thee to the depth and breadth and
                        height

Double-space between lines

                    My soul can reach, when feeling out of
                        sight

Single-space and indent runover
lines 5 spaces.
Double-space to next line

                    For the ends of Being and ideal Grace.

                    I love thee to the level of everyday's

                    Most quiet need, by sun and candle-
                        light

                    I love thee freely, as men strive for
                        Right;

                    I love thee purely, as they turn from
                        Praise

                    I love thee with the passion put to use

                    In my old griefs, and with my childhood's
                        faith.

                    I love thee with a love I seemed to lose

                    With my lost saints,--I love thee with
                        the breath,

                    Smiles, tears, of all my life!--and, if
                        God choose,

                    I shall but love thee better after death.

GREETING CARDS

Greeting cards make up a multibillion dollar international industry that gets bigger every year. (Just when you thought there was no new subject or occasion for which you could buy a greeting card, a new category is likely to be invented.) Although most greeting card companies employ people to create their specific messages, freelance writers are encouraged to submit material.

As with any other type of manuscript, greeting cards are presented in certain generally recognized formats and are submitted via certain generally recognized methods.

On the following pages, you will find valuable information that will help you find the best way to submit your copy and to keep track of your submissions. You'll also find tips on how to request guidelines from card companies and how to type a variety of greeting card messages.

Typing and Size of Submission

Type each verse on a separate piece of paper. Full-size paper (8½"x11"), half sheets, or 3"x5" or 4"x6" *cards* are all acceptable. Most writers submit verse on 3"x5" cards; however, studio-card producers sometimes request 9"x9½" folded-paper submissions.

Verse is generally typed double-spaced, but if necessary, you can use single spacing.

If you have a title for the verse, center the heading and type it in capital letters.

Your Name and Address

Type your name and address in the left-hand corner (or on the back of the card) of *each* submission (the cards can accidentally get scattered).

Create a Code

To keep up with your submissions (and sales), you should create a unique coding system. Number each card in the right-hand corner. Create your own numbering system with code numbers or alphabet codes. These can be your own initials and a number, the company initials and a number, or another such code. But make it simple— and write down your code in your duplicate-card file.

Illustration Ideas

Submit illustration ideas on a separate page, clipped to the appropriate verse.

Send for Greeting Card Company Guidelines

The guidelines are necessary to understand the company's approach, needs, and *taboos*.

Send for names and addresses of greeting card companies (Artist and Writers Market, ℅ The Greeting Card Association, 1356 New York Ave., NW, Suite 615, Washington, DC, 20005), or consult *Artist's Market* or *Writer's Market* (Writer's Digest Books). If the guidelines do not specify the number of submissions, send five ideas—and make them your best ones!

Keep Records

Keep records in a 3"x5" card file that holds duplicates of your submissions. Group ideas by subject, season, one-liners, prose, verse, and so on.

SAMPLE LETTER—
Requesting list of
greeting card
producers

Your name, address;
single-spaced if typed.

Simple one-line OK

Use business format—block
form.

Include stamped, self-addressed
envelope.

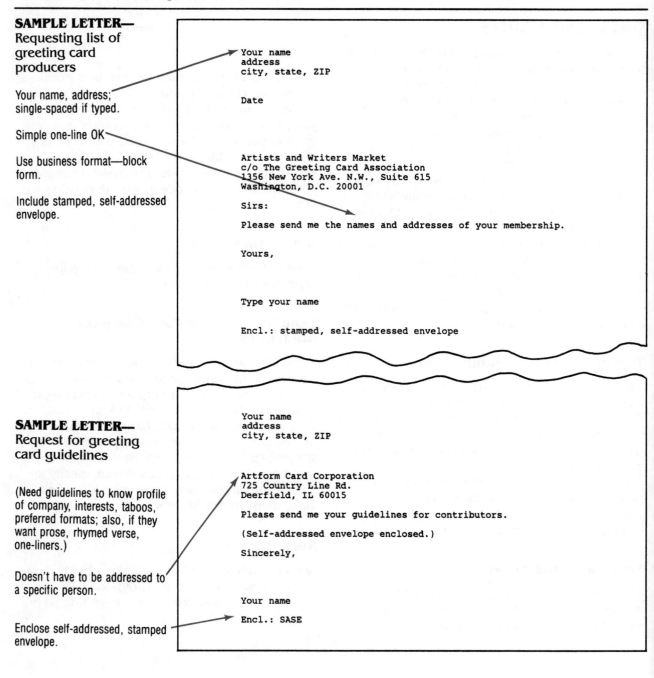

```
                    Your name
                    address
                    city, state, ZIP


                    Date




                    Artists and Writers Market
                    c/o The Greeting Card Association
                    1356 New York Ave. N.W., Suite 615
                    Washington, D.C. 20001

                    Sirs:

                    Please send me the names and addresses of your membership.


                    Yours,



                    Type your name


                    Encl.: stamped, self-addressed envelope
```

SAMPLE LETTER—
Request for greeting
card guidelines

(Need guidelines to know profile
of company, interests, taboos,
preferred formats; also, if they
want prose, rhymed verse,
one-liners.)

Doesn't have to be addressed to
a specific person.

Enclose self-addressed, stamped
envelope.

```
                    Your name
                    address
                    city, state, ZIP


                    Artform Card Corporation
                    725 Country Line Rd.
                    Deerfield, IL 60015

                    Please send me your guidelines for contributors.

                    (Self-addressed envelope enclosed.)

                    Sincerely,



                    Your name

                    Encl.: SASE
```

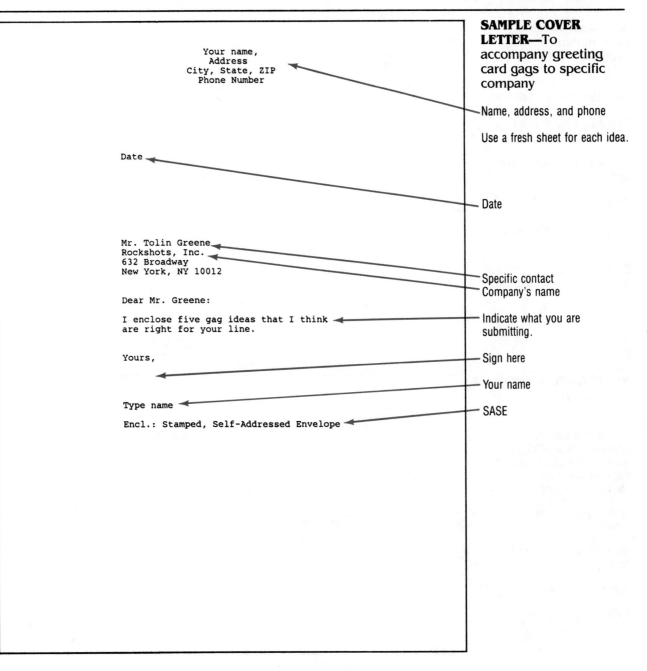

Your name,
Address
City, State, ZIP
Phone Number

Date

Mr. Tolin Greene
Rockshots, Inc.
632 Broadway
New York, NY 10012

Dear Mr. Greene:

I enclose five gag ideas that I think
are right for your line.

Yours,

Type name

Encl.: Stamped, Self-Addressed Envelope

SAMPLE COVER LETTER—To accompany greeting card gags to specific company

Name, address, and phone

Use a fresh sheet for each idea.

Date

Specific contact
Company's name

Indicate what you are submitting.

Sign here

Your name

SASE

SAMPLE—General
presentation of
greeting card idea

Use either 3"x5" or 4"x6" card.

Type each verse or idea on a
separate card.

Double-space verse if space
permits.

Center and capitalize title.

Create number system for each
card.

Single-space name and address
(name can be on back of card).

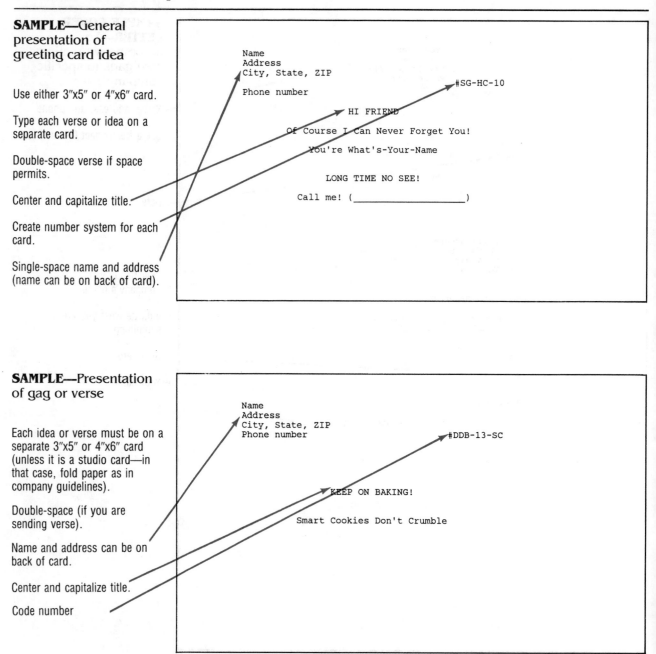

```
Name
Address
City, State, ZIP                        #SG-HC-10

Phone number

                        HI FRIEND
            Of Course I Can Never Forget You!
            You're What's-Your-Name

                LONG TIME NO SEE!

            Call me! (_____)
```

SAMPLE—Presentation
of gag or verse

Each idea or verse must be on a
separate 3"x5" or 4"x6" card
(unless it is a studio card—in
that case, fold paper as in
company guidelines).

Double-space (if you are
sending verse).

Name and address can be on
back of card.

Center and capitalize title.

Code number

```
Name
Address
City, State, ZIP                        #DDB-13-SC
Phone number


                KEEP ON BAKING!

            Smart Cookies Don't Crumble
```

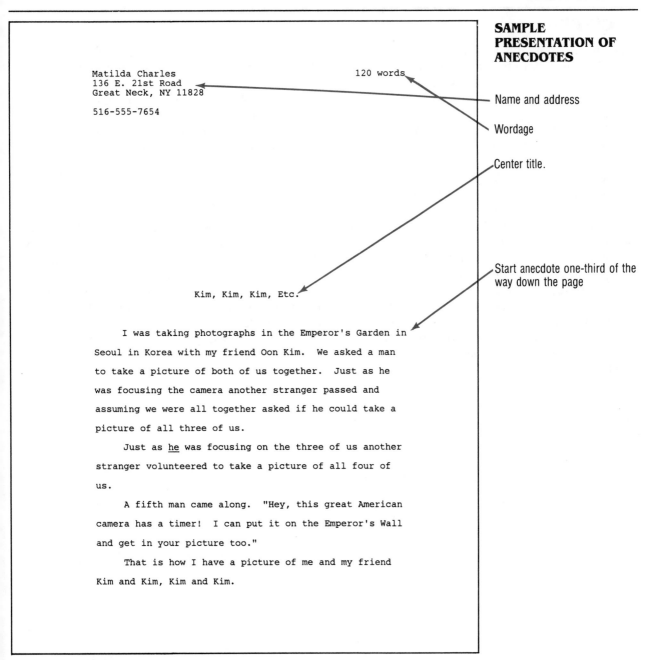

Matilda Charles
136 E. 21st Road
Great Neck, NY 11828

516-555-7654

120 words

SAMPLE PRESENTATION OF ANECDOTES

— Name and address

— Wordage

— Center title.

— Start anecdote one-third of the way down the page

Kim, Kim, Kim, Etc.

I was taking photographs in the Emperor's Garden in Seoul in Korea with my friend Oon Kim. We asked a man to take a picture of both of us together. Just as he was focusing the camera another stranger passed and assuming we were all together asked if he could take a picture of all three of us.

Just as <u>he</u> was focusing on the three of us another stranger volunteered to take a picture of all four of us.

A fifth man came along. "Hey, this great American camera has a timer! I can put it on the Emperor's Wall and get in your picture too."

That is how I have a picture of me and my friend Kim and Kim, Kim and Kim.

ANECDOTES

An anecdote is a very special kind of story. Originally, anecdotes related some facts of history or recounted a folk story or legend in a short, concise format. Later, the anecdotal form was also used to tell an amusing story about oneself or someone else.

The important difference between an anecdote and other story-telling devices such as books or short stories is that it tells its story in as brief a form as possible. However, as short as it is, the reader should come away with a feeling that she or he has heard a *complete* story.

RECIPES

The recipe market is a far better filler market than hints or tips. Here are the rules:

1. Send for a style sheet. Each magazine may list ingredients and level measurements in a different fashion.

2. Present your recipe in both paragraph form and in order of use. The paragraph can be from 30 to 120 words long and should include complete cooking and mixing instructions as well as occasion for serving the food. If this isn't your own recipe, tell where you got it. If you are entering a recipe contest, send for the guidelines and follow the rules *exactly*.

3. Pay attention to how you use words. Terminology is important. Follow the style of the magazine (or contest). Do they present the directions at the beginning or the end of the recipe? Do they use the word *tools, materials,* or *supplies?* Do they use the word *instructions* or *directions?*

4. All ingredients, tools, and supplies must be listed in the order of use.

5. List the temperature and length of cooking, as well as the amount of time for cooling, if necessary.

6. Indicate an approximate number of portions or servings.

7. Review: Can you shorten or simplify the directions? For clarity, should you add to the instructions? Is each word you are using precise?

Recipe Contests

You may be a cook who prefers a ''pinch'' and a ''handful''—one who cooks by instinct and by eye. But if you want to win a contest, you must be exact in your use of terminology, in the steps, and in the directions. Even the address of the contest is important. You can be disqualified for any deviation from the rules.

Send for contest guidelines. If there are no precise directions for a recipe format, here is one you can follow.

WRITING THE RECIPE FOR A CONTEST

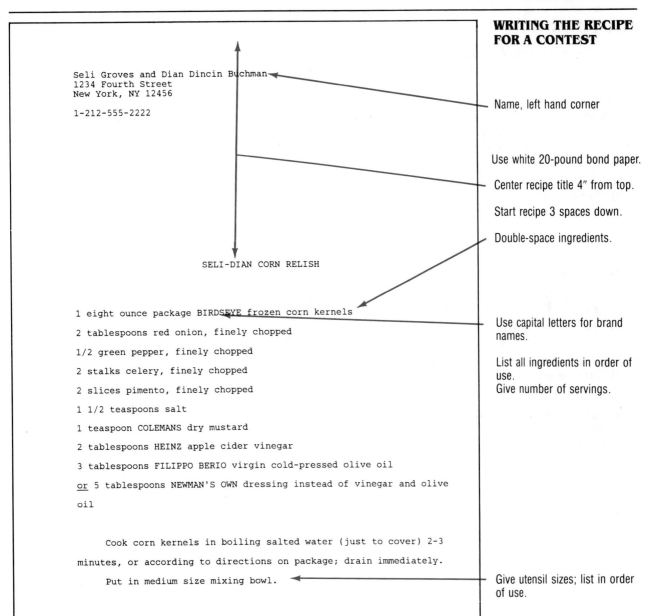

Seli Groves and Dian Dincin Buchman
1234 Fourth Street
New York, NY 12456

1-212-555-2222

Name, left hand corner

Use white 20-pound bond paper.

Center recipe title 4″ from top.

Start recipe 3 spaces down.

Double-space ingredients.

SELI-DIAN CORN RELISH

1 eight ounce package BIRDSEYE frozen corn kernels

2 tablespoons red onion, finely chopped

1/2 green pepper, finely chopped

2 stalks celery, finely chopped

2 slices pimento, finely chopped

1 1/2 teaspoons salt

1 teaspoon COLEMANS dry mustard

2 tablespoons HEINZ apple cider vinegar

3 tablespoons FILIPPO BERIO virgin cold-pressed olive oil

or 5 tablespoons NEWMAN'S OWN dressing instead of vinegar and olive
oil

Use capital letters for brand names.

List all ingredients in order of use.
Give number of servings.

        Cook corn kernels in boiling salted water (just to cover) 2-3
minutes, or according to directions on package; drain immediately.
        Put in medium size mixing bowl.

Give utensil sizes; list in order of use.

PHOTOGRAPHY

Everyone knows photographers are special people. Whether they use simple box cameras or the most elaborate setups, they have a knack for using light to help create visual statements.

Well, we have a special knack, too. We can help turn your systems of submission, coding, filing, and retrieval into simple-to-follow methods.

With the tips and checklists found in Et Cetera (pages 175-77), you need never again have to worry about lost photos or misfiled negatives.

You'll know exactly what you sent out and to whom, how many were bought, how many were retained, and how much you're getting paid.

In this section we'll show you how to prepare a query letter, a release form for consent to use someone's name or picture, a photographer's résumé, and a cover letter.

Once you've started to use the suggestions made in this section, handling your precious photographs will be a snap.

Photographer's Résumé

On occasion, you may need to present a brief résumé of your photographic background and experience. Do not complicate matters by including everything you have ever done. Stick to the important (and photographic) highlights. Prepare the résumé in advance; enclose a copy if it is relevant to your query.

Information to Include in a Résumé
Area of Experience
For example, industrial, on set for movies, editorial, advertising, staff (list place or places).

Publications
List pertinent magazines, books, newspapers, audio visual aids, advertising promotion pieces, other areas.

Education
(Optional—include if relevant)

Specific photography-related education
Include important workshops.

Exhibitions and/or shows
Name, place, date (most recent is listed first).

Awards, achievements

Professional memberships

Your Letterhead
Name
Address
City, state, ZIP

Phone number

_____

TO:

_____

_____

_____

_____

Date

_____

QUERY:

Preparing Your Query Letter
- Introduce yourself.
- Briefly describe your photographs.
- Mention your specialty (if you have one).
- Indicate variety of photographs; include stock list of available photographs.
- If asking about an assignment or proposing a photo story, indicate how you will fulfill assignment.
- Give publication credits (name only the most important or pertinent). If many, list them on a separate sheet and enclose with query.
- If including photographs with query, don't use a self-mailer like the one above. Send three or four representative blowups from your contact sheet. Never send original transparencies; send good duplicates instead. Request return of photographs. Always include a return envelope with adequate postage. Include a self-addressed

SAMPLE—Query letter
(self-mailer—outside)

fold in

REPLY:

fold here

fold here

Used for query and reply; not to
include photos

Have these forms printed on 2
sides of an 8½″x11″ sheet

LOVE
USA 22

Your Name

Address

City, State, ZIP

postcard requesting acknowledgment of receipt
of photographs.

- Enclose résumé (if needed).

Cover Letter Acknowledging Sale

- Include *invoice* with name, address, city, state,
  zip code number, and title or description of
  photographs.

SAMPLE RELEASE FORM—
Consent to use of name or picture

This is one example of a model release. Styles will vary. Check *Photographer's Market* for additional release information.

Special clause concerning fee may be necessary (e.g., "For the sum of $_____, I hereby irrevocably consent . . .").

Block form, single-spaced

Center on page.

Date_____

I hereby irrevocably consent that my name and/or any picture or portrait of me, or of any part of me, and reproductions thereof, or pictures of_____, may be used by _____ for such purposes as (s)he may desire in connection with his/her research, writing, and professional activities, and may be used, exhibited, and published through any medium whatsoever as part of or in connection with his/her research, writing, and professional activities, even though such use may be for advertising purposes or purposes of trade.

I hereby certify and represent that I am (am not) over 21 years of age.

Name _____

Address _____

City _____ State _____ ZIP _____

Signature _____

***

CONSENT OF PARENT OR GUARDIAN

(To be obtained when person signing above is
under 21 years of age)

I,_____, am the parent/guardian of_____, and I hereby irrevocably consent that his/her name and/or any picture or portrait of him/her or any part of him/her and reproductions thereof, may be used by _____ for such purposes as s/he may desire in connection with his/her research, writing, and professional activities, and may be used, exhibited, and published through any medium whatsoever as part of or in connection with his/her research, writing, and professional activities, even though such use may be for advertising purposes or purposes of trade.

Signature_____

Name_____

Address_____

Release Forms for Photographers

One of the most important housekeeping items in a photographer's operation is having the right type of release prepared for use when needed. It's not enough to have people say it's all right to take their picture and then assume you can use that picture any way you like: using someone's likeness for any commercial reason usually means having to get permission first. And that means having a generally accepted release form executed by the photographer and the subject.

PART 3

Scripts

If it's on screen, on stage, or in a forum—wherever people are being entertained or informed, chances are somebody wrote a script for it first.

In the pages ahead, you'll find information basic to all scripts plus samples and diagrammed formats of scripts for soap operas, comedy formats, teleplays, audio-visual scripts, screenplays, and stage plays. This section deals with several different types of scripts: Television, Film, Audio-Visual, and Plays.

SECTION 1: TELEVISION SCRIPTS

Just about everything you see and hear on television is scripted. Even talk shows aren't as impromptu as the medium would like you to believe. Guests are pre-interviewed by the show's staff, who then provide the host with a list of questions or leading comments. Nor are game shows entirely spontaneous. The quick wit of the host is helped by jokes and observations written by *his* staff after they've interviewed the contestants and reviewed their audition tapes.

But it takes more than a gift for turning a dramatic or comedic phrase to sell a script to television. Many a worthy idea never made it to the TV screen because the writer—as talented as he or she may be—didn't know what a treatment was, or how to prepare one, or even how to set the typewriter margins.

Time and space in television have applications Albert Einstein never reckoned with: a script not only has to be written to fit a certain amount of time but it must also follow certain space requirements, including specifications for margins, dialogue placement, and other elements.

Different types of shows require specific formats, but there are basic rules applicable to most TV scripts. For those who use computers, various formatting software programs are available. These can usually work with the software you already have. For example, *PowerText, Smartkey,* and *PowerPerfect,* among others, make it possible for you to use a minimum of keystrokes to create perfect formats for the medium you're writing in.

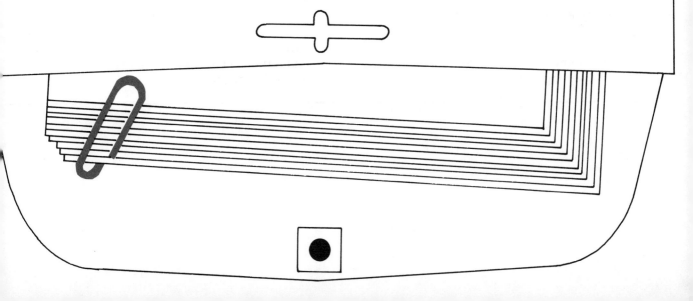

Many of the popular programs can also be easily adapted for use in script writing. *WordPerfect 4.1*, for example, has some very good column features. (Column movements are the key to setting up the spacing for a scripting format.) Another important capability of a computer is keeping track of the number of times characters appear in a series. This feature is especially important for daytime soap operas because the frequency of airing (five times a week) can make it easy for the writing team to lose track of the characters' appearances. The risk of overexposing the character has nothing to do with dramatic effect; it's strictly budgetary. Many actors sign for a guaranteed minimum number of appearances for which they are paid; if they appear more often, they must be paid accordingly. The scriptwriter must be careful not to go over that minimum without permission from the producer.

Something to keep in mind when you approach script writing is the basic difference between scripts and other literary efforts: Books and magazine articles are meant to be *read*. Scripts, even if they're never produced, are meant to be *acted*. This basic characteristic of scripts is one reason format is so important: it tells the camera how to shoot the action; it tells the stage manager how to place the players; and it tells the actors what to say and when to say it—and even *how* to speak the speech they're given.

For television, the concept of time is another imperative. Knowing how to write a script so that it meets the time constraints of the medium is essential.

The following charts provide easy-to-read guides to setting margins, using upper- and lower-case type, and figuring time usage.

Script Format for TV

The first thing to do is set your typewriter margins. All settings here are in *pica* type. Do not use elite. If you work with a computer, do not use a dot-matrix printer. Your software manuals will guide you in setting margins and tabulations. (Text formatters, as noted earlier, make this process much easier.)

Your top and bottom margins should be about an inch deep *except* for situation comedies, in which top and bottom margins should be at least an inch and a half. The added white space is needed for notes. The left margin should be as wide as possible for easier reading in a binder.

The general rule for scripts is to bind them so that they can lie flat when being read. Your local print shop or copy shop may have this service. Professionals most often use glossy, vinyl stock with gold embossed title and name. The title is centered. Your name and address, or your name, your agent's name and address are placed in the lower right hand corner of the cover.

If you decide to bind your manuscript there is an exceptional and reliable script typing service used by television studios, screenwriters and playwrights: Studio Duplicating Service, Ken Shaw, Manager, 446 West 44th Street, New York, NY 10036. Phone: 212-563-1225. They can give you a rough estimate on the phone, and state their exact fee after they see the script. The charges depend on length of script, number of copies needed, how messy and indecipherable the script is (they even take handwritten scripts) and the cost of the cover.

If you prefer to type your own script but want a professional looking binder, Studio Duplicating Service can emboss your title and your name and address on your preferred choice vinyl cover, and mail it to you with the brass screw hardware closures. They send it out for next day delivery.

Also, it is quite acceptable today to type your own script and place it in a 2- or 3-hole binder with a metal clasp. And remember: Never send your original copy.

AT-A-GLANCE GUIDE TO TV SCRIPT FORMAT

Margin Settings for Most TV Scripts

FADE IN—15

Left margin—15

Right margin—75

Dialogue (left margin)—25

Dialogue (right margin)—55

Dialogue instructions in parentheses

Character's name (above dialogue)—40

Transition guides, e.g., FADE OUT—66

Page number—72 in upper right margin

Camera, stage, and scene directions—left margin, 15; right margin, 55

Camera shot subject—20

Narrative links—60

Words to Capitalize in a TV Script

ACT ONE, ACT TWO, ACT THREE (etc.)

Location of scene (e.g., MARRAKESH DOCKSIDE)

Parenthetical directions of how lines are delivered

SUBJECT of camera shot

EXT. (the commonly used abbreviation for *exterior*)

INT. (the commonly used abbreviation for *interior*)

NIGHT (at heading of scene)

DAY (at heading of scene)

MORE

CONT'D

ACT

SHOW closing

Character's NAME (always place above the dialogue)

NEW character (brought in via narrative)

Sounds (for example: GUNSHOT; THUNDER CLAP)

SCENE descriptions

CAMERA DIRECTIONS

STAGE DIRECTIONS

CAMERA SHOTS

Line Spacing

Single-space

Dialogue, narrative

Character directions

Descriptions of scenes

Camera directions

Stage directions

Sound or effects cues

Double-space

Between different characters' speeches

Between lines of dialogue

Between character's name and subject of shot

Between narrative and character's name, scene or camera shot, or subject of following shot

(Instructions on dialogue delivery) in parentheses. This is typed two lines below character's NAME.

Slug or header

Generally not used, because scripts should be bound.

Timing

It's almost impossible to write to fit the exact split second. And even if you did, the actor can add or subtract seconds from your script by the way he/she reads the lines. But you can write to fit certain set timing guides that allow for the variables that occur. The following are *approximations* that come close to the mark:

W.P.S.—words per second

20 words = 10 seconds

45 words = 20 seconds

65 words = 30 seconds

130 words = 60 seconds

Approximate timing for outlines and scripts

10-15 pages in outline = ½ hour

20-25 pages in outline = 1 hour

25-40 pages in outline = 1½ hours

45-60 pages in outline = 2 hours

1 page of script = 50-52 seconds

3 pages of script = 2½ minutes

10 pages of script = 9-10 minutes

30 pages of script = ½ hour

60 pages of script = 1 hour

125-128 pages of script = 2 hours

The number of pages in relation to time can vary depending on the format used; in TV writing, the format is *one-column* or *two-column*. In addition, *business* (the term used to describe bits of action, such as "John scratches his nose") must be put into the script and can affect the page count.

The First Step: The Treatment

The first step in selling a television script (or teleplay) is to prepare a *treatment,* which contains details such as: characters, scenes, locations, plot devices, act breaks, indications of specific dialogue (voice-overs, asides, etc.), climax, and some direction for the cameras, e.g., MOVE IN ON. A treatment can run from fifteen to fifty pages, and is, basically, your story told scene by scene in the present tense.

One good way to avoid *treatment phobia,* an affliction that nips many a budding scriptwriter, is to think of it as telling a friend a long story about an experience you had; but when writing, you must convert all characters into third person and place them in the present tense.

For example, for the treatment, you wouldn't say: *I ran from the burning building after it exploded and found him waiting for me.* Instead, you would write: *Mary runs from the burning building and finds John waiting for her.*

Many writers come a cropper in the detail department. Train yourself to *see* everything in your mind's eye as completely as possible. Use that technique to transfer these recaptured details to the treatment when you write it.

The Outline

An outline is a shorter version of the treatment, containing just characters, act breaks, scenes, locations, plot devices, and climax. Most outlines for half-hour scripts run seven to fifteen pages. They're skeletons that are fleshed out in the script.

Note: Most writers send outlines or treatments along with finished scripts. Agents and producers are more likely to read the shorter versions of a work first and if they find these of interest, go on to the script itself.

(For more information on agents, see Et Cetera, pages 154-55.)

Pitching

The word *pitching,* in the writer's lexicon, means throwing out ideas and hoping they'll be caught and returned with a contract for a sale. Some people think of the pitch as an oral presentation of an idea. That misunderstanding may come from the fact that pitches are thrown during brainstorming sessions. If a pitch is ever thrown at any other time, chances are good that the potential catcher won't even try to pick up the toss, and for very good reason. Prudence, acting in behalf of both the writer and the potential buyer, dictates that at all times everything is to be presented in written form only. This practice protects both the writer, whose idea might be deliberately or inadvertently used without proper credit or recompense, and the producer, who may be accused of having stolen a spoken idea. Therefore, when you think of a pitch, think of it as words on paper—otherwise, you might strike out without ever reaching the batter's box.

In essence, whether you offer a concept, a synopsis, a storyline—or go the more traditional (and accepted) way and present an outline, treatment, or even a completed script—it's basically all a pitch. The difference lies in the length of each presentation and the degree of detail each includes.

Regardless of how long or short the presentation is, a good way to practice making your pitch effective is to imagine it in the hands of a very busy producer who has only a few minutes to spare. If you can give the essence of your idea in three to five sentences, you are halfway to first base.

Incidentally, sometimes a producer or her or his associate may find a script so extraordinary that she helps prepare the writer to orally "pitch" the essence of the script in a conference where development money is being discussed. (Development money is something like an advance given to an author.)

Most writers submit outlines or treatments. A new writer might submit an outline or treatment along with a finished script. Only a certain group—the V.W.E.Ws. (Very Well Established Writers)—can sometimes sell a producer on the basis of a concept or theme around which a script or show can be written. In most instances, writers submit a synopsis or storyline. Following are examples of all three methods:

Concept pertains to a *series* as a whole, *not to any script in particular.* Here's a sample of how a concept for a mythical series, *Gilda's Girls,* might begin:

> *GILDA JONES, a mystery woman, suddenly appears in town and sets up an agency with beautiful models who work as undercover police agents. They operate under cover of the modeling assignments they assume around the world. They get involved in dangerous situations and in romantic relationships, sometimes with the villains, sometimes with the good guys. (Etc.)*

Storyline—A *storyline* is a slightly expanded version of the concept. However, it pertains to *a specific script* for a series. It runs two pages—certainly no more than three. A storyline contains the basic conflict, the names of the major characters, plot crisis, and the windup or climax. Example:

> *GILDA is upset at the way MAVIS has been acting and begins to suspect that she may be a double agent. The only one who can confirm or disprove this is RICK, who has disappeared without telling anyone where he's going.*

Synopsis—The *synopsis* is the shortest offering of all: it presents the basic theme of a *completed script.* It should be, ideally, just a few lines. A synopsis of Poe's *The Pit and the Pendulum,* for example, might be:

> *A man waits helplessly as a sharp scimitar swings closer and closer to him as it descends from some unseen place above him. Just as he's about to be sliced in two, something unexpected happens.*

Sample Format for Title Page of Television Script

The following is an example of a typical title page for a script. This can also be adapted for use with an outline and/or a treatment. If it is to be used for a treatment, be sure to insert the words *A TREATMENT* in all caps, centered two single-spaces below the title.

SAMPLE—Television
script title page

(If this is a treatment, add
words A TREATMENT 2 lines
below title.)

Title: 20 single-spaces from top
of page—centered—all caps,
bracketed in quotes, and
underlined.

Drop 4 lines;
center;
type in upper- and lower-case.

Drop 2 lines;
center;
type writer's name in upper- and
lower-case.

If your script is based on
another work—a book, play,
etc.—drop 8 lines after your
name and type derivation and
author.

Lower left corner, 2 inches from
bottom: DRAFT NUMBER and
date submitted, single-spaced.
Lower right corner, 2 inches
from bottom, type your or your
agent's name, address, phone
number, single-spaced, upper-
and lower-case.

*Note: Top lines of bottom two
entries start on the same line.*

                    "GILDA'S GIRLS"

                     Written by

          Seli Groves and Dian D. Buchman

          Based on the play A Model Woman

                    by Jane Jones

THIRD DRAFT   Delia Ware
May 1, 1988   A. B. WARE AGENCY
                                         722 E. 22 St.
                                         Troy, New York
                                         515-555-4444

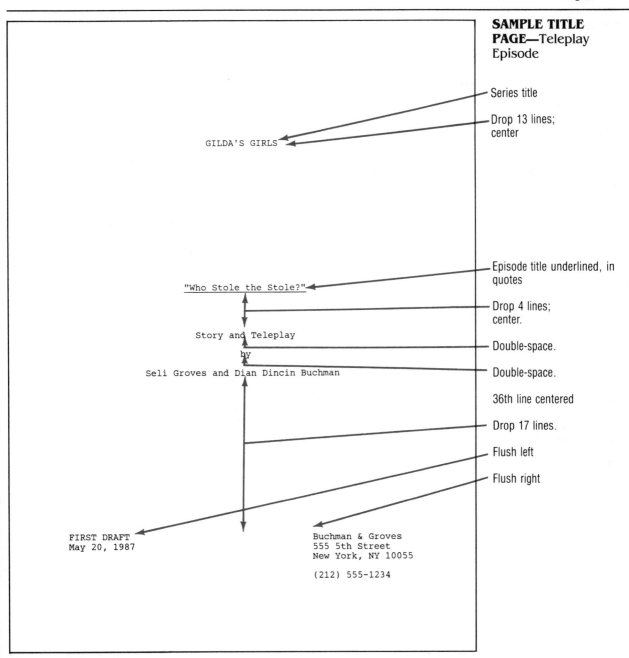

SAMPLE TITLE PAGE—Teleplay Episode

Series title

Drop 13 lines; center

GILDA'S GIRLS

Episode title underlined, in quotes

"Who Stole the Stole?"

Drop 4 lines; center.

Story and Teleplay

Double-space.

by

Double-space.

Seli Groves and Dian Dincin Buchman

36th line centered

Drop 17 lines.

Flush left

Flush right

FIRST DRAFT
May 20, 1987

Buchman & Groves
555 5th Street
New York, NY 10055

(212) 555-1234

TELEPLAYS

By definition, a *teleplay* is a story written in a format suitable for conversion to the TV medium. It contains dialogue, scene descriptions, sound effects, and camera directions. Most writers who write teleplays produce basic one-hour scripts for episodic series.

An *episodic series* revolves around one or more characters who are involved in the series on a continuing basis. This means that the writer has to know not only how to write a teleplay, but also how to make sure it conforms to the theme of the series as a whole. In other words, there are three C's to be aware of: *creativity* (regardless of what you may have heard about television writing, the really good writers do produce highly original work); *conformity* (to the format, that is); and *continuity*—making sure that you know the theme of the series you're writing for.

SAMPLE—Teleplay in one-column format

Set left margin at 40; right margin 75. Type descriptions in CAPS, and single-space.

Large left margin for director's notes

Drop 2 lines for sound effects, upper-case, underlined, single-space.

Drop 2 lines; double-space.

Drop 2 lines; single-space.

Drop 2 lines. (CU is abbreviation for closeup.)

Drop 2 lines.

Dialogue delivery CAPS, parentheses, underlined

Drop 2 lines; underline and CAP sound

Transition

FADE IN ON THE WAREHOUSE, LOCATED AT THE END OF A DEAD-END STREET. SHOW BROKEN WINDOWS ON EXTERIOR. FOLLOW NANCY AND NED INTO A DARK AND DUSTY INTERIOR. NANCY AND NED LOOK APPREHENSIVE AS THEY SEARCH THROUGH A CLUTTER OF OLD BOXES AND WRAPPING MATERIALS ON THE FLOOR.

<u>SOUNDS OF CARS ON THE ROAD OUTSIDE --LOUD ROCK MUSIC IS HEARD FROM AN ADJOINING ROOM.</u>

NANCY WHEELS AROUND. <u>(GASPS)</u>: I think I might have kicked something.

CAMERA MOVES TO WIDER SHOT OF NANCY. NED CROSSES TO HER.

CU NED.

NED <u>(SHAKY VOICE)</u>: I hope it was your own ankle.

<u>SQUEAKY DOOR CREAKS OPEN.</u>

FADE TO BLACK.

There are one- and two-column TV scripts for teleplays. The two-column format presents both the video and audio (the sights and the sounds) of a teleplay separately—one in each column of the page. A script written in the one-column format, on the other hand, alternates descriptions of video and audio. Most directors prefer the one-column format, since it leaves them room to make notes and indicate camera changes as they see fit.

SAMPLE—Teleplay in two-column format

VIDEO and AUDIO heads are caps, underlined.

Tab in to 15 to begin VIDEO column; 40 to begin AUDIO column.

VIDEO directions upper-case, single-spaced.

AUDIO sound effects upper-case, single-spaced, underlined.

AUDIO character name and how line is read upper-case, underlined; in parentheses.

Camera directions in VIDEO column, upper-case.

Transition under VIDEO is upper-case.

<u>VIDEO</u>
FADE IN ON THE WAREHOUSE LOCATED
AT THE END OF A DEAD-END STREET.
SHOW BROKEN WINDOWS ON EXTERIOR.
FOLLOW NANCY AND NED INTO A DARK
AND DUSTY INTERIOR. NANCY AND NED
LOOK APPREHENSIVE AS THEY SEARCH
THROUGH A CLUTTER OF OLD BOXES
AND WRAPPING MATERIALS ON THE FLOOR.

NANCY WHEELS AROUND.

CAMERA MOVES TO WIDER SHOT OF NANCY.
NED CROSSES TO HER.

CU NED.

SQUEAKY DOOR CREAKS OPEN.

FADE TO BLACK.

<u>AUDIO</u>
SOUNDS OF CARS ON THE ROAD
OUTSIDE -- LOUD ROCK MUSIC
IS HEARD FROM AN ADJOINING
ROOM.

NANCY (GASPS): I think

I might have kicked some-

thing.

NED (SHAKY VOICE): I hope

It was your own ankle.

TV COMEDY FORMATS (SITCOMS)

Most TV comedies are thirty minutes long. They're usually made up of two acts and an end tag. Acts usually run three scenes each. Because most TV comedies use a three-camera setup, it's unnecessary, and almost impossible, to give camera directions in the script. Leave it to the director to call the shots.

An important point for writers: Before submitting an outline, treatment, or script for a series, watch the series over a period of time to pick up such basics as characterizations, settings, and tempo. While many writers will write lines that are true to the characters' personalities and will gear their scripts in time with the show's usual pacing, they sometimes forget that most shows confine the action to the same sets each time. Therefore, avoid having your action take place outside of any of the show's standing sets.

And whatever you do, don't neglect the major characters. There's a story about a novice writer who submitted a funny script for the old *I Love Lucy* series. The trouble was that most of the hilarious action took place between Fred and Ethel, the writer's favorite characters. It wasn't accepted. But the postscript is that the writer reportedly recast his characters, giving the same funny situations now to Ricky and Lucy. You guessed it—it was accepted.

AT-A-GLANCE GUIDE TO TV COMEDY FORMATS

Margin settings	Camera and stage directions—Left 15; Right 55
	Scene descriptions—Left 15; Right 55
	Dialogue—Left 25; Right 55
Name of the character speaking	Type in upper case, centered above his or her lines.
Description of how the speech is to be read	Set margins left 25; right 55. Type in parentheses two lines below the name of the character speaking.
Single-space	Camera and stage directions
	Scene descriptions
	Cues for effects
Double-space	Transitions from scene headings between character's name above dialogue and directions or descriptions
	Between scene headings and first lines of directions or scene descriptions
	Between character's name and dialogue
	Between dialogue lines
	Between dialogue and directions or scene descriptions

Between dialogue and transitional guides

Between description and transitional guides

Between transitional devices and act or closings.

Use Upper Case	ACT HEADINGS
	EXT. or *INT.*
	ALL DIRECTIONS
	SPEECH DELIVERY (e.g., *LAZILY*)
	TRANSITIONS
	TAGS
	DAY OR NIGHT
	CLOSINGS—ACT and SHOW
	ALL DESCRIPTIONS
	CHARACTER NAMES (except when part of dialogue)
	MORE or *CONT'D* (used to show how character's dialogue continues from preceding page or to following page)
Underline	Sound effects; camera, stage, and scene directions

NOTES

When writing for television, it's important to become familiar with the way cameras are used. You can take courses that teach these techniques and/or you can learn more about them through books that teach technical TV writing.

Usually, scripts for movies, TV, radio, and theater are submitted by authors' agents. In order to protect themselves from potential plagiarism charges, producers refuse to open any unagented material. (See Agents, pages 154-55.)

Scripts for TV comedy series are usually written to fit the thirty-minute time format.

A typical script has two *acts* and a *tag*. Each *act* has three scenes. The *tag* is the device that provides commentary on the preceding material. You may remember *Hill Street Blues* or see reruns of the police drama from time to time. Usually each script would wind up with two of the main characters, Captain Furillo and Joyce Davenport, discussing for about two minutes what happened in that episode. In a mystery show, such as *Murder, She Wrote*, the tag usually has the sleuth, Jessica Fletcher, adding a little extra insight into how she solved the case. In a comedy series, such as *The Cosby Show*, Dr. and Mrs. Huxtable are usually shown relaxing and discussing their latest triumph in parenting or recalling another funny incident related to the one their family just went through.

On the next page, we've set up a sample title page for a TV comedy. It contains a Scene/Page indicator so that anyone going through the script can quickly find the scene he or she wants to work with at the time.

**TV COMEDY
FORMAT (SITCOM)—**
Title page

20 lines down (series name)

22 lines down (show name)

25 lines down

27 lines down

32 lines down: scene and page
indicators, which make it easy
to find specific scenes that will
be worked with at a given time;
double-space.

51st line

```
                        THE DIAN & SELI SHOW

                        "Mix-Up at Morty's"

                        Written by

                        Timothy Charles


                        SCENE - PAGE NO.

                             A - 1

                             B - 9

                             C - 20




                                      Represented by:

                                      Jay Jones Agency
                                      777 West 57 Street
                                      New York, NY 10077
                                      1-212-555-5555
```

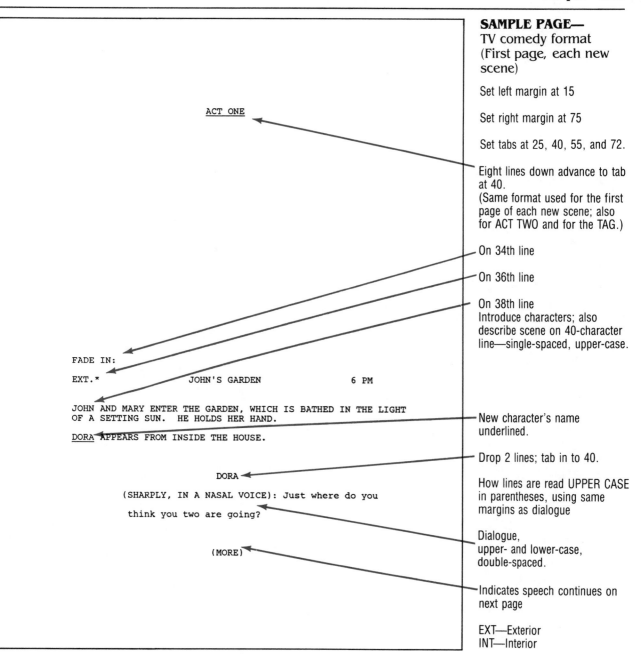

ACT ONE

FADE IN:

EXT.*   JOHN'S GARDEN   6 PM

JOHN AND MARY ENTER THE GARDEN, WHICH IS BATHED IN THE LIGHT
OF A SETTING SUN. HE HOLDS HER HAND.

DORA APPEARS FROM INSIDE THE HOUSE.

                    DORA

          (SHARPLY, IN A NASAL VOICE): Just where do you

          think you two are going?

                    (MORE)

SAMPLE PAGE—
TV comedy format
(First page, each new
scene)

Set left margin at 15

Set right margin at 75

Set tabs at 25, 40, 55, and 72.

Eight lines down advance to tab
at 40.
(Same format used for the first
page of each new scene; also
for ACT TWO and for the TAG.)

On 34th line

On 36th line

On 38th line
Introduce characters; also
describe scene on 40-character
line—single-spaced, upper-case.

New character's name
underlined.

Drop 2 lines; tab in to 40.

How lines are read UPPER CASE
in parentheses, using same
margins as dialogue

Dialogue,
upper- and lower-case,
double-spaced.

Indicates speech continues on
next page

EXT—Exterior
INT—Interior

SAMPLE PAGE—TV comedy (sitcom) format continued

Dialogue—typed on 30-character line.

Tab in to 40.

Tab in to 66.

[Start a new page for the next scene.]

```
                    DORA (CONT'D)
          (ANGRILY): You two have no sense of
                  responsibilty.
                          JOHN
          (STEPS IN FRONT OF MARY AND FACES DORA): I
            wouldn't want your (SNEERINGLY) kind of
          responsibility because you're responsible for
            everything that goes wrong around here.

                                        TRANSITION TO
```

SAMPLE PAGE—First page of new scene of any ACT or TAG

Left margin is at 15.

```
FADE IN:

INT.              MARY'S LIVING ROOM            DAWN THE NEXT DAY
MARY IS SITTING ON A STOOL, HER ARMS WRAPPED AROUND HER KNEES.
MAVIS ENTERS CARRYING A CUP.  SHE CROSSES TO MARY, WHO LOOKS UP
STARTLED.


                        MAVIS
        (WARMLY) I had a feeling you might like a cup of tea.

                        MARY
        (SMILES, NODS) You're right.  As usual.  God.  (SIGHS)

        Bless whoever invented this stuff.


                                        FADE OUT


                    END OF ACT ONE
```

Backspace from right margin at 75.

On line 28

On line 31

A new character is shown in upper-case, underlined.

Drop 2 lines after dialogue; tab in to 40.

Tab in to 25.

Centered and underlined in CAPS

SOAP OPERAS

Daytime soap operas began on radio in the 1920s and moved into television in 1950. Technically, the radio soap *Big Sister* was on TV in 1946, but only on an experimental basis. In 1947, a series called *A Woman to Remember* aired for a short while. In 1951, *Search for Tomorrow* debuted; it lasted through December 1986. (See Jean Rouverol's *Writing for the Soaps* [Writer's Digest Books], also Seli Groves' *History of America's Daytime Dramas* [Contemporary] for a history of this genre, as well as instructional help.)

Today, the soaps (called that because they were originally owned by soap manufacturers who produced them and used them as advertising vehicles) provide the networks with 70 percent of their income. They've come a long way from the early live fifteen-minute-a-day productions. Most of them are now one hour long; are taped and edited daily, using the same production values found in night-time productions; and use well-made sets, specially designed wardrobes, and location shooting.

But as multi-Emmy winner Douglas Marland (head writer at various times of such soaps as *General Hospital, Guiding Light, As the World Turns,* and *Loving*) told the authors: "While viewers appreciate all these *extras,* what they really want is a good story."

Paul Rausch, who created the soap *Texas,* and who has been executive producer of many daytime dramas, including *Another World* and *One Life to Live,* sums up the basic secret of a soap's success: "Story, story, story."

How the Story is Told

A typical soap writing team consists of some eight persons. The head writer or head writing team produces a *bible,* which is also called the *book* or the *projection.* This contains the basic story themes that will be followed over a period of several months to two years. When the bible is approved by the executive producer, the network, and the production company (who in some cases may own the soap, as in the case of Procter and Gamble, which owns *Another World, As the World Turns,* and *Guiding Light*) the head writers then break down the projection into both weekly and daily outlines. These are then given to the other members of the writing team, called the dialogue writers, who write dialogue based on the breakdowns.

In many TV scripts, camera directions are indicated by the writer; however, in soaps, the director is the one who will set up the camera angles.

A head writer works for the network or production company that owns the soap. A dialogue writer works for a head writer and is usually paid out of the head writer's fees.

The authors have created a soap (for purposes of this book only!) called *Days of My Children's Lives.* Besides listing ourselves as head writers, we have also indicated a team of dialogue or associate writers as well as a slate of other personnel. Except for the authors, all of these staff members are fictional.

The following pages show how a typical daily breakdown and script would look.

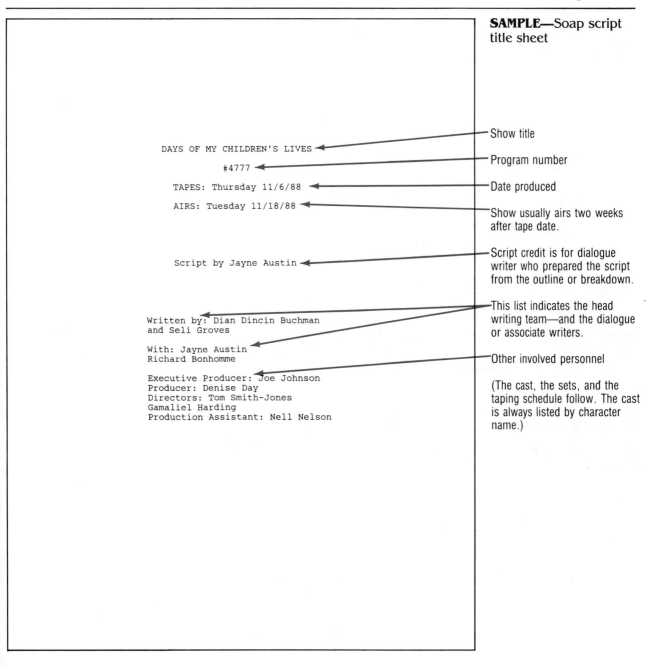

SAMPLE—Soap script title sheet

DAYS OF MY CHILDREN'S LIVES — Show title

#4777 — Program number

TAPES: Thursday 11/6/88 — Date produced

AIRS: Tuesday 11/18/88 — Show usually airs two weeks after tape date.

Script by Jayne Austin — Script credit is for dialogue writer who prepared the script from the outline or breakdown.

Written by: Dian Dincin Buchman and Seli Groves

With: Jayne Austin Richard Bonhomme

This list indicates the head writing team—and the dialogue or associate writers.

Executive Producer: Joe Johnson
Producer: Denise Day
Directors: Tom Smith-Jones
Gamaliel Harding
Production Assistant: Nell Nelson

Other involved personnel

(The cast, the sets, and the taping schedule follow. The cast is always listed by character name.)

SOAP SCRIPT—Cast, sets, and taping schedule

Single-space cast and sets.

Triple-space schedule; type in 2 columns.

Actors go through their paces using their scripts.

The director works out the actors' movements on the set.

The executive producer and director will make changes as they see fit. The writers incorporate these changes into the script.

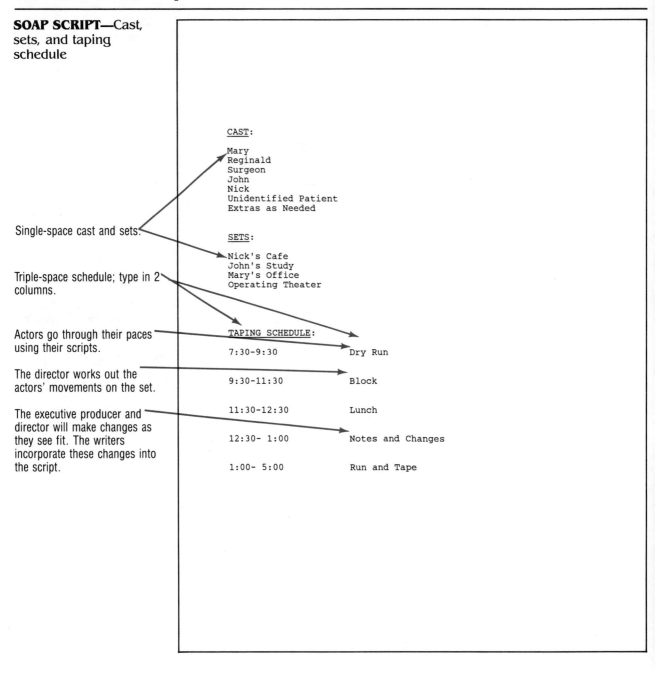

```
                        CAST:

                        Mary
                        Reginald
                        Surgeon
                        John
                        Nick
                        Unidentified Patient
                        Extras as Needed


                        SETS:

                        Nick's Cafe
                        John's Study
                        Mary's Office
                        Operating Theater


                        TAPING SCHEDULE:

                        7:30-9:30              Dry Run

                        9:30-11:30             Block

                        11:30-12:30            Lunch

                        12:30- 1:00            Notes and Changes

                        1:00- 5:00            Run and Tape
```

SAMPLE—Soap script
teaser

Set needed

Cast needed

TEASER A: NICK'S CAFE (REGINALD and EXTRAS)   Same Day

Reginald is holding a letter and begins to understand that Mary
won't give up her beloved shoe business for him.

CUT TO:

TEASER B: MARY'S OFFICE (MARY, JOHN)

John is looking into Mary's eyes. She is looking at Reginald's
picture on her desk. Tears form in her eyes. She begins to
wonder if being the most famous woman in the shoe business is
worth giving Reginald the boot.

CUT TO:

TEASER C: OPERATING ROOM (SURGEON, EXTRAS)

The doctors and nurses stand around the operating table.
Remember: we don't yet know who the patient is. Have the
personnel discuss the strange circumstances by which the injured
person was brought into the hospital.

GO TO BLACK

SAME DAY: (This means: If the action took place on Wednesday afternoon in the story the day before, it's still Wednesday afternoon as the writer starts the script.)

TEASERS are the next direction given by the head writers to the dialogue writers.

This direction indicates that the viewer will see his or her TV screen go blank.

Teasers

These are the opening scenes of each day's episode. They often pick up where the previous day's
action left off. These scenes are considered the
most important, since they're designed to make
the audience stay tuned for the rest of the show.

Triple-space between acts.

ACT ONE A: NICK'S CAFE (JOHN, REGINALD, NICK, EXTRAS)
Continue, but not directly, from the last episode. Show John
watching Reginald sitting at one end of the bar. Have John call
a waiter to his table and give him a written message for
Reginald. Have Reginald read the message and indicate his mood
change from curiosity to anger. He flashes around, sees John,
and clenches his fists. What the hell does John think he's
doing? Have John laugh in his face. Show him enjoying the
torment he's putting Reginald through. Nick enters.

CUT TO:

ACT ONE B: MARY'S OFFICE (MARY ON PHONE)
She's using a falsely bright voice while talking to a buyer from
Oshkosh, Wisconsin. When she hangs up, she looks at Reginald's
picture and buries her head in her hands. She opens the top
drawer in her desk and reaches for a gun. Under her breath, she
talks about taking drastic action to correct an error.

CUT TO:

ACT TWO A: OPERATING THEATER (SURGEON, EXTRAS)
The surgeon calls for readings on the patient's condition. One
of the nurses gasps as the surgeon makes an incision.

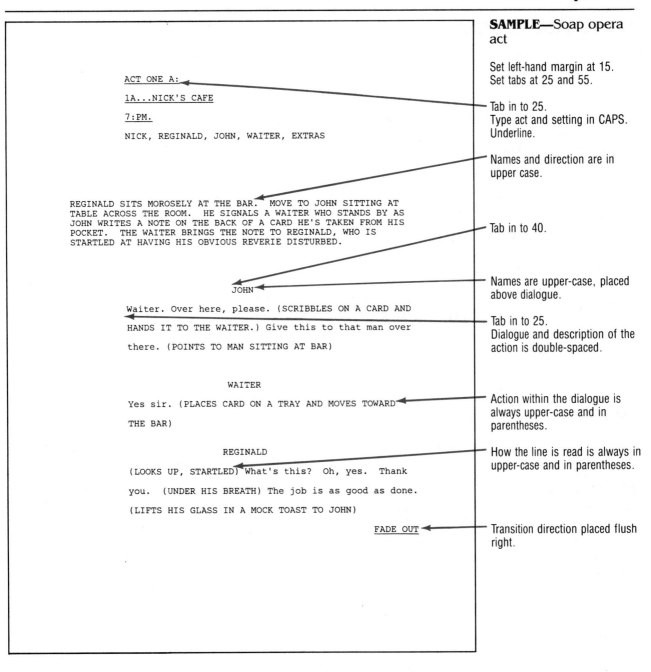

ACT ONE A:

1A...NICK'S CAFE

7:PM.

NICK, REGINALD, JOHN, WAITER, EXTRAS

REGINALD SITS MOROSELY AT THE BAR. MOVE TO JOHN SITTING AT
TABLE ACROSS THE ROOM. HE SIGNALS A WAITER WHO STANDS BY AS
JOHN WRITES A NOTE ON THE BACK OF A CARD HE'S TAKEN FROM HIS
POCKET. THE WAITER BRINGS THE NOTE TO REGINALD, WHO IS
STARTLED AT HAVING HIS OBVIOUS REVERIE DISTURBED.

                        JOHN

Waiter. Over here, please. (SCRIBBLES ON A CARD AND

HANDS IT TO THE WAITER.) Give this to that man over

there. (POINTS TO MAN SITTING AT BAR)

                    WAITER

Yes sir. (PLACES CARD ON A TRAY AND MOVES TOWARD

THE BAR)

                    REGINALD

(LOOKS UP, STARTLED) What's this? Oh, yes. Thank

you. (UNDER HIS BREATH) The job is as good as done.

(LIFTS HIS GLASS IN A MOCK TOAST TO JOHN)

                                    FADE OUT

Set left-hand margin at 15.
Set tabs at 25 and 55.

Tab in to 25.
Type act and setting in CAPS.
Underline.

Names and direction are in
upper case.

Tab in to 40.

Names are upper-case, placed
above dialogue.

Tab in to 25.
Dialogue and description of the
action is double-spaced.

Action within the dialogue is
always upper-case and in
parentheses.

How the line is read is always in
upper-case and in parentheses.

Transition direction placed flush
right.

AUDIO-VISUAL SCRIPTS

The audio-visual market is expanding all the time. Writers are finding this a very lucrative area in which to work.

Audio-visual presentations are used to train sales forces. They're also used to assist doctors in learning about new products or procedures. They're an essential part of an advertising agency's TV-commercial format.

Essentially, an audio-visual production needs: (1) a script and (2) some sort of on-screen presentation. The latter can be a film, or an animated feature, or just a series of mats on which the message is spelled out. In many cases, the scriptwriter prepares V.O. (voice-over) copy, which an off-camera actor or narrator reads in connection with the film, animation, or illustration on screen.

AT-A-GLANCE GUIDE TO AUDIO-VISUAL SCRIPTS

Cover Sheet

CAPITALIZE	TITLE, REEL, NETWORK (OR COMPANY) NAME, DATE OF DRAFT, CAST, WRITER, OTHER PRODUCTION PERSONNEL, LOCATION, TAPE DATE
Upper and lower case	All other data
Spacing	Single-space—except between names, directions, etc.

Script Page

Top	Repeat project title, network number, reel number. Indicate new page number.
Camera-shot number placement	At left side of video column *and* on right side of audio column. Numbers for specific camera shots are always on the same line, e.g., Number 1A at left of the video column will appear directly across from number 1A at right of audio column.
Margins	Set at 15 for video.
	Tab in to 40 for audio.
Capitalize	Video, audio, directions (KEY, O.C., V.O., SOT*, etc.)
Underline	*Speaker* whether indicated by V.O. or O.C.
Spacing	*Single-space* video copy except between numbered camera shots or other directions (KEY, etc.).
	Double-space audio copy.

*O.C. stands for *on camera;* V.O. stands for *voice-over;* SOT stands for *sound on tape.*

| Timing | Indicate at bottom right corner time elapsed per page over total time elapsed for all pages up to that point. Type this as you would a fraction. See sample, page 134. |

Remember this timely, and timeless, tip: Always write a few words short of your outside time limit. It's much easier for a narrator to *stretch* to fill time than it is for an editor to have to cut seconds out of a tape later on. The scriptwriter who not only writes well but also writes within a defined time limit is someone who can be expected to receive priority consideration when assignments are handed out.

Ten Tips for Successful Audio-Visual Writing

As competition heats up for this increasingly important and well-paying medium, an audio-visual scriptwriter needs information to give him or her an added advantage in the field. Some tips gleaned from the most successful writers follow:

Think of your writing as speaking. Use short sentences and words more likely to be heard than read.

Listen to what you write. Dictate your script to yourself using a cassette recorder. After you've written, read it aloud. Ask someone to record it and listen to how another voice interprets it.

Think of yourself as writing a newspaper piece. That means using the inverted pyramid, in which the essential who, where, when, how, and why facts are up front and the rest is commentary.

Limit each scene to no more than fifteen seconds. Just as with other on-screen media, the more movement, the better. Call for different camera angles or shots if there's no other way to break up a long scene.

Cut away from talking heads as quickly as possible. Nothing's more boring than to see closeups of heads for more than a few seconds.

Remember the authors' KISS tip for your audio-visual copy: Keep it Short and Simple. Good word choice makes even the most complex issues easier to understand.

Go for drama. Just because you're talking about a way to size fabric, for example, doesn't mean you can't choose exciting sound effects and visuals.

Use transitions whenever possible: verbal and/or visual changes add interest.

Consult frequently with your director to make sure you can get the most effective camera angles possible.

REPEAT—REPEAT—REPEAT. People tend to remember what has been repeated frequently; that is why commercials always repeat the name of the product and why composers repeat musical passages throughout their works. Always try to refer several times to an important point in your copy.

Audio-Visual Script for Educational Film

This audio-visual script sample is a revised version of a film made by a pharmaceutical company for video cassettes to be used by doctors.

These scripts can be written so that they are followed (played) by the people involved. Camera angles are called for, and close-ups (CUs) and long shots are determined, before actual filming or taping begins. Doing this is especially important where the possibility of a lot of talking heads or the sweep of a panel shown for several minutes at a time would make for a dull production. Therefore, the experienced writer would know when to call for such techniques as different camera angles and shots of different areas around the room.

Often, the scripts are written after the fact. The writer watches the raw footage. The director, often in tandem with an experienced writer, decides what to keep and what to cut, and the production

SAMPLE—Audio-Visual
cover sheet

Time indication centered

Left margin is set at 15.
Right column begins at 40.

Indent 6 spaces from edge of
right column.

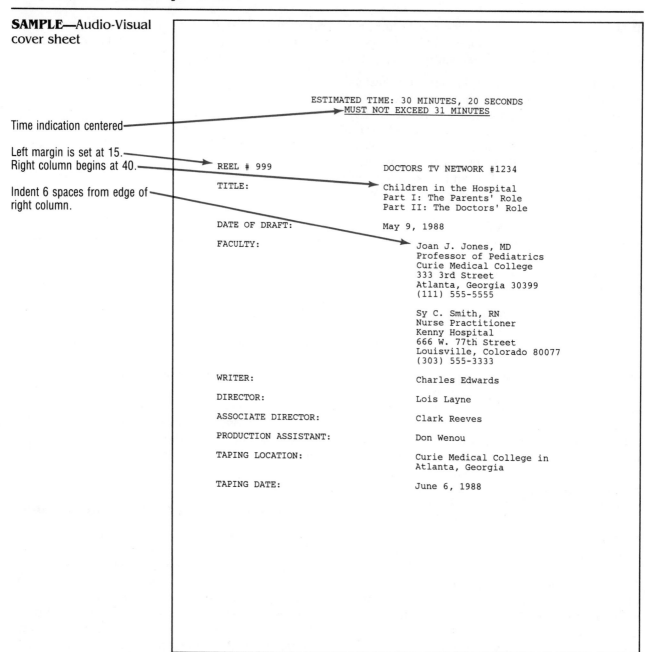

```
                              ESTIMATED TIME: 30 MINUTES, 20 SECONDS
                              MUST NOT EXCEED 31 MINUTES


      REEL # 999                        DOCTORS TV NETWORK #1234

      TITLE:                            Children in the Hospital
                                        Part I: The Parents' Role
                                        Part II: The Doctors' Role

      DATE OF DRAFT:                    May 9, 1988

      FACULTY:                          Joan J. Jones, MD
                                        Professor of Pediatrics
                                        Curie Medical College
                                        333 3rd Street
                                        Atlanta, Georgia 30399
                                        (111) 555-5555

                                        Sy C. Smith, RN
                                        Nurse Practitioner
                                        Kenny Hospital
                                        666 W. 77th Street
                                        Louisville, Colorado 80077
                                        (303) 555-3333

      WRITER:                           Charles Edwards

      DIRECTOR:                         Lois Layne

      ASSOCIATE DIRECTOR:               Clark Reeves

      PRODUCTION ASSISTANT:             Don Wenou

      TAPING LOCATION:                  Curie Medical College in
                                        Atlanta, Georgia

      TAPING DATE:                      June 6, 1988
```

script is written to fit that footage.

A cover sheet and several pages of a script are
shown here, beginning with the cover sheet
above. These samples will be shown with explanations and as they would appear if actually used.

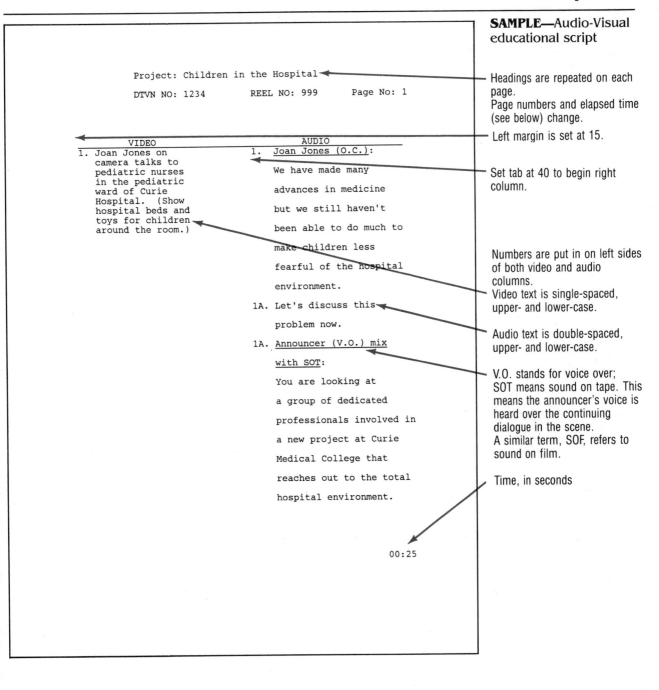

SAMPLE—Audio-Visual educational script

Project: Children in the Hospital

DTVN NO: 1234   REEL NO: 999   Page No: 1

VIDEO	AUDIO
1. Joan Jones on camera talks to pediatric nurses in the pediatric ward of Curie Hospital. (Show hospital beds and toys for children around the room.)	1. Joan Jones (O.C.): We have made many advances in medicine but we still haven't been able to do much to make children less fearful of the hospital environment.
	1A. Let's discuss this problem now.
	1A. Announcer (V.O.) mix with SOT: You are looking at a group of dedicated professionals involved in a new project at Curie Medical College that reaches out to the total hospital environment.

00:25

Headings are repeated on each page.
Page numbers and elapsed time (see below) change.
Left margin is set at 15.

Set tab at 40 to begin right column.

Numbers are put in on left sides of both video and audio columns.
Video text is single-spaced, upper- and lower-case.

Audio text is double-spaced, upper- and lower-case.

V.O. stands for voice over; SOT means sound on tape. This means the announcer's voice is heard over the continuing dialogue in the scene.
A similar term, SOF, refers to sound on film.

Time, in seconds

**SAMPLE
PAGE**—Audio-Visual
educational script
(continued)

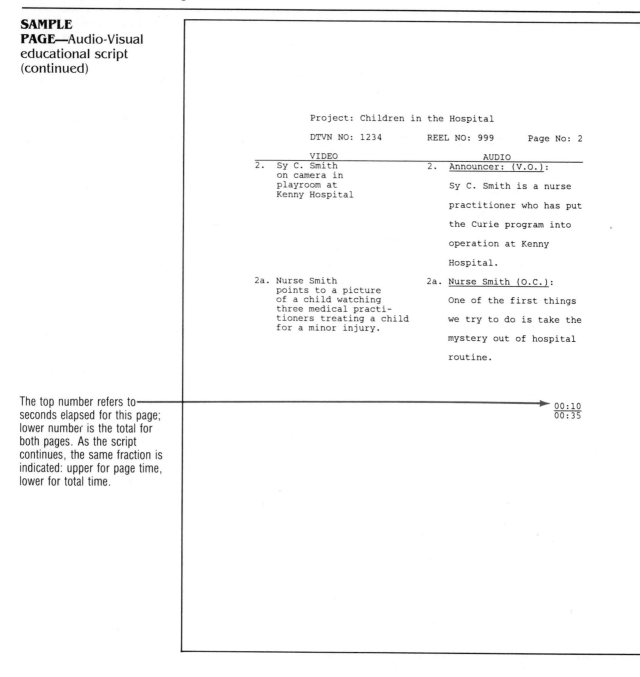

Project: Children in the Hospital

DTVN NO: 1234   REEL NO: 999   Page No: 2

VIDEO	AUDIO
2. Sy C. Smith on camera in playroom at Kenny Hospital	2. Announcer: (V.O.): Sy C. Smith is a nurse practitioner who has put the Curie program into operation at Kenny Hospital.
2a. Nurse Smith points to a picture of a child watching three medical practitioners treating a child for a minor injury.	2a. Nurse Smith (O.C.): One of the first things we try to do is take the mystery out of hospital routine.

00:10
00:35

The top number refers to seconds elapsed for this page; lower number is the total for both pages. As the script continues, the same fraction is indicated: upper for page time, lower for total time.

SCREENPLAYS

Many of the techniques used for television films are similar to theatrical film scriptwriting. The dividing line between the two media continues to fade, especially since edited versions of the same production may appear both in theaters and on TV. However, distinctions do remain, and we'll deal with them in the following pages.

One important difference, however, is that movies for theatrical release—that is, for movie houses—are shot on film. Some television productions are shot on tape. The latter is easy to work with and weighs far less when it comes to shipping tapes around the country or the world. The former, however, gives superior production-oriented results: There is more depth to film. Actors like the way they look on film. Some writers will say they even prefer to write for film, although that preference may lie more in the tendency to like the visual result rather than any influence it may have on the writing itself.

And, speaking of writers, let's discuss how screenwriters actually produce those scripts that get sold to the movie moguls. The usual course to follow is this:

First, a treatment, or outline, needs to be developed. This is always written in present tense. As in the case of television outlines or treatments, this takes the form of a story describing everything from the idea and on through each and every scene. All the characters are described; their relationships to and with each other are discussed; and the ways and means by which the action proceeds are detailed. Where a writer finds it important to do so, suggestions may be made on how to use the camera at certain points, e.g., *as Jane reads the contract, the camera picks up the tears that well up in her eyes.*

A treatment can run from ten to one hundred pages, but the norm seems to be about fifteen to sixty pages.

For most new writers, selling the treatment may be the only link between their work and the final screenplay that emerges. This is because most producers prefer to use screenwriters who know their craft well to develop the script from the treatment. But even these seasoned professionals don't always have their work accepted the first, or second, or third, or whatever time. (But they're usually well paid for each draft and sometimes even get screen credit for their work.)

Some directors, such as the late Alfred Hitchcock, insist on a fully-scripted production before they allow so much as a cue light to be turned on. Others are known to rewrite the script as they shoot. Indeed, sometimes the final version of a screenplay has about as much resemblance to the writer's first submission as Charlemagne has to Prince Charles: so many generations of drafts exist that while a skilled genealogist could link the ancestor to the descendant, he or she would have to wade through a pretty well-muddled script gene pool.

The next important thing for a new screenwriter to remember is that film producers are really astute businessmen and they don't like to waste time. One sure giveaway that they may be about to deal with a complete tyro and, hence, a potential time-waster, is to be presented with a treatment or outline or script that doesn't follow the recognized and accepted format.

Keep the following At-a-Glance Guide handy as you go through the formats that follow. You'll be able to refer to it quickly to make comprehension of the sample pages easier.

AT-A-GLANCE GUIDE TO SCREENPLAYS

Camera shots	Number; type on both left and right margins. e "heading" line.

Margins

Scene numbers	Left 15; right, 75
Camera directions and scene descriptions	Left, 20; right, 73
Dialogue and character name	Left, 30; right, 68

The character's name is typed in UPPER-CASE, and is placed above the dialogue lines. Descriptions of how the character speaks (*lazily, quickly, earnestly*) are set in parentheses below the character's name and to the left of it.

Use Upper-case for	*INT.* or *EXT.* at scene heading WHERE THE SCENE IS SET THE TIME OF DAY OR NIGHT CHARACTERS' NAMES CAMERA DIRECTIONS SCENE TRANSITION DEVICES
Single-space	Dialogue Camera directions Scene descriptions Stage directions Cues
Double-space	From camera shot to camera shot Between scene and FADE IN, FADE OUT, DISSOLVE TO Between dialogue and new character headings Between dialogue and stage or camera direction

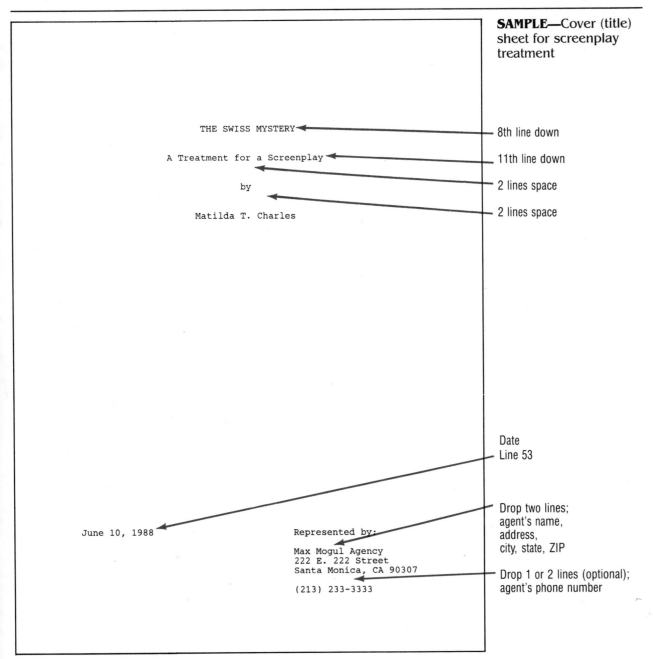

SAMPLE—Cover (title) sheet for screenplay treatment

THE SWISS MYSTERY ◄—————— 8th line down

A Treatment for a Screenplay ◄—————— 11th line down

◄—————— 2 lines space

by

◄—————— 2 lines space

Matilda T. Charles

Date
Line 53

Drop two lines;
agent's name,
address,
city, state, ZIP

June 10, 1988   Represented by:

Max Mogul Agency
222 E. 222 Street
Santa Monica, CA 90307

Drop 1 or 2 lines (optional);
agent's phone number

(213) 233-3333

SAMPLE—Screenplay treatment page

8th line, centered

11th line, centered

13th line, centered
15th line, centered

19th line
Set margins on 15 and 73.
Indent paragraphs.

Double space

Type characters' names in upper-case when first mentioned and in upper- and lower-case thereafter.

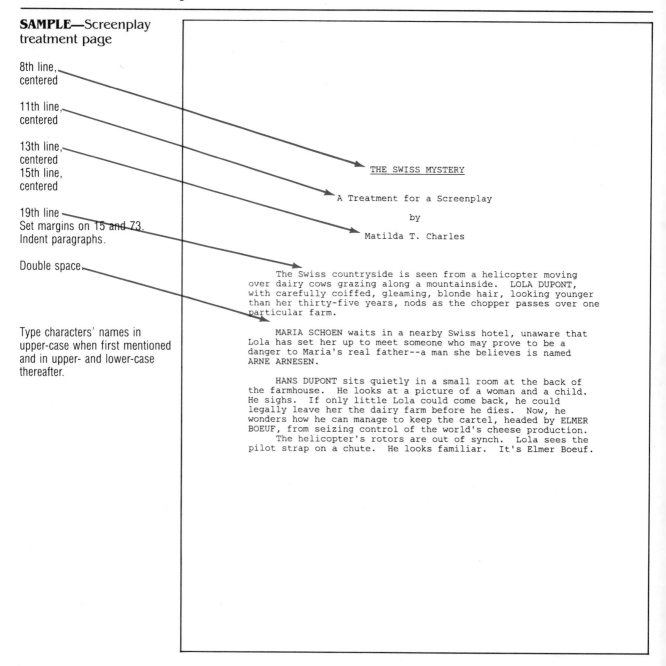

THE SWISS MYSTERY

A Treatment for a Screenplay

by

Matilda T. Charles

        The Swiss countryside is seen from a helicopter moving over dairy cows grazing along a mountainside. LOLA DUPONT, with carefully coiffed, gleaming, blonde hair, looking younger than her thirty-five years, nods as the chopper passes over one particular farm.

        MARIA SCHOEN waits in a nearby Swiss hotel, unaware that Lola has set her up to meet someone who may prove to be a danger to Maria's real father--a man she believes is named ARNE ARNESEN.

        HANS DUPONT sits quietly in a small room at the back of the farmhouse. He looks at a picture of a woman and a child. He sighs. If only little Lola could come back, he could legally leave her the dairy farm before he dies. Now, he wonders how he can manage to keep the cartel, headed by ELMER BOEUF, from seizing control of the world's cheese production.
        The helicopter's rotors are out of synch. Lola sees the pilot strap on a chute. He looks familiar. It's Elmer Boeuf.

SAMPLE—Title page
for a screenplay

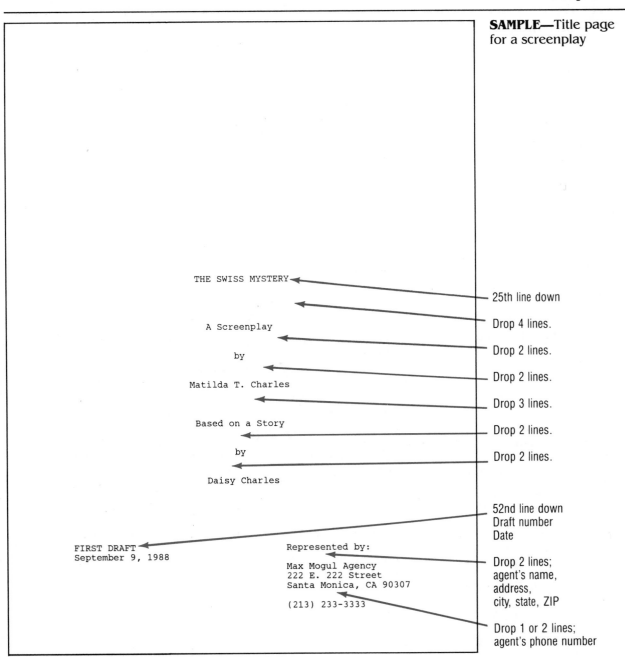

THE SWISS MYSTERY ← ————————— 25th line down

———————— Drop 4 lines.

A Screenplay ← ————————— Drop 2 lines.

by ← ————————— Drop 2 lines.

Matilda T. Charles

———————— Drop 3 lines.

Based on a Story ← ————————— Drop 2 lines.

by ← ————————— Drop 2 lines.

Daisy Charles

52nd line down
Draft number
Date

FIRST DRAFT
September 9, 1988

Represented by: ← ————————— Drop 2 lines;
agent's name,
Max Mogul Agency   address,
222 E. 222 Street   city, state, ZIP
Santa Monica, CA 90307

(213) 233-3333

———————— Drop 1 or 2 lines;
agent's phone number

SAMPLE—Screenplay page

Left margin, 15
Right margin, 75

7th line;
Caps and underlined

12th line
Indent 20 spaces.
Camera shot

14th line
Indent 15 spaces.
Camera shot number at left,
same shot number at right

DESCRIPTIONS of setting,
characters are in caps,
single-spaced.
Indent 30 spaces.

Backspace from right margin,
type transitional guides
upper-case in parentheses.

Tab in to 40;
type name of character

If dialogue is continued on next
page, use this device; avoid
breaking dialogue if possible.

INT. or EXT. in caps

Slant lines indicate scene
continues

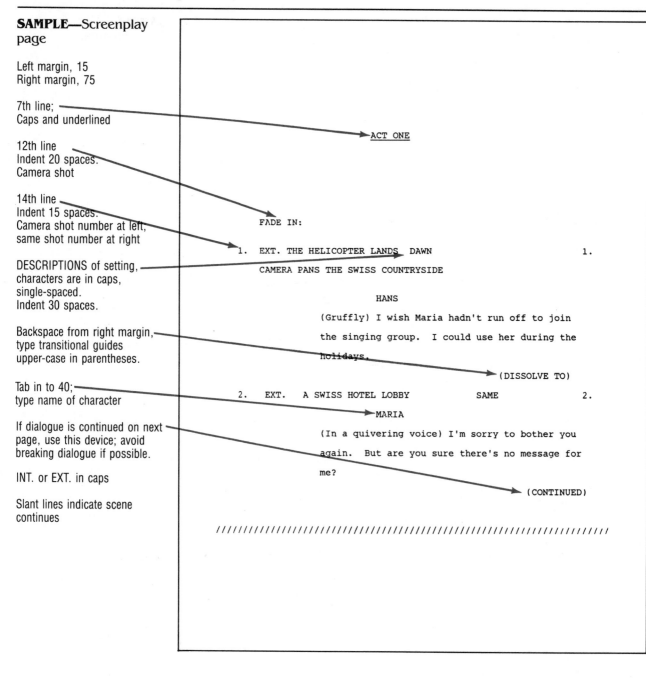

```
                                        ACT ONE


                      FADE IN:

      1.   EXT. THE HELICOPTER LANDS  DAWN                        1.
           CAMERA PANS THE SWISS COUNTRYSIDE

                              HANS
                      (Gruffly) I wish Maria hadn't run off to join
                      the singing group.  I could use her during the
                      holidays.
                                              (DISSOLVE TO)
      2.    EXT.    A SWISS HOTEL LOBBY           SAME            2.
                      MARIA
                      (In a quivering voice) I'm sorry to bother you
                      again.  But are you sure there's no message for
                      me?
                                              (CONTINUED)


      ///////////////////////////////////////////////////////////////
```

PLAYS

We can't tell you how to write a play. It may well be one of the most difficult forms of communication between people. There are no fancy camera shots to help in making transitions; no close-ups; no retakes. The playwright depends on his or her writing talent and on the actors and directors who will make the work come alive.

But before that play can be produced, it must be bought. And that means it must be presented in the proper format.

On the following pages we will show you a portion of a real playwright's work. Ms. Ronnie Paris has had her plays produced over the years, and when you see, even by this small excerpt, how well she develops her characters and plotlines as she moves through the work, you can understand the importance of obeying the *primary rule* for playwriting: polish, polish, polish.

Before discussing Ms. Paris's play, *The Killing Time,* we would like to give you some basic crafting tips you must know in order to present a professional-looking manuscript.

Plays are generally presented in paper binders that allow the play to be opened and read flat. Use a 2- or 3-ring spring binder or inexpensive metal clasp binder such as Duo Binder. Attach a simple white label on the outside cover to identify it. Include the title of the play and your name. Playwrights can also use the more expensive vinyl covers described under screenplays.

"Make it easy for the producer to read your play," cautions Mary Carlin, literary associate for the non-profit membership group, New Dramatists. She says the most common problems in presentation are small margins, dull and indistinct type and ribbon, and bad spelling mistakes. She also reminds playwrights to allow many spaces between the character's name and the start of the dialogue.

Place the page numbers in the upper right corner and number sequentially. However, if you have numbered each act separately, include a slug or header with the *act number.* This is particularly important with plays because they are often taken apart for photocopying to be read by different people.

The New Dramatists invites five new dramatists into its organization each year. Send for applications to 424 West 44th Street, New York, NY 10036.

Two useful resource books: *Playwright's Handbook,* Thomas Dunn (NAL) and *Dramatists Source Book,* TCG (Theatre Communications Group), 355 Lexington Avenue, New York, NY 10017.

AT-A-GLANCE GUIDE TO PLAYWRITING FORMAT

Paper	Because plays tend to be "worked" a great deal when they're read, it's important to use good 16- or 20- pound bond paper.
Margins	Be generous. Allow at least 1¼" at the top and bottom. (An extra ½" wouldn't hurt.) Allow a left margin of 1½". Some people say 1¼" is enough, but we say, give the manuscript that extra quarter inch. It will look nicer when it's put in the binder. The right margin should be at least an inch.
Capitalize	Characters' names, which are set over the dialogue.
Descriptions	Include action, how a character speaks, etc., which are placed in parentheses.
Stage Directions	Place in parentheses.
What Follows Title Sheet	Well, it's not the play, but it's a very important part of your manuscript. It's a separate page on which you list your characters, the setting, the time of year, time of day, etc.

PLAY TITLE PAGE

No page number on title page

22 lines down

Centered;
caps

Drop 4 lines.

Drop 4 lines.

53rd line
Skip 2 lines between author's
phone number and agent's
name.

Copyright line is on same line as
agent's phone no.

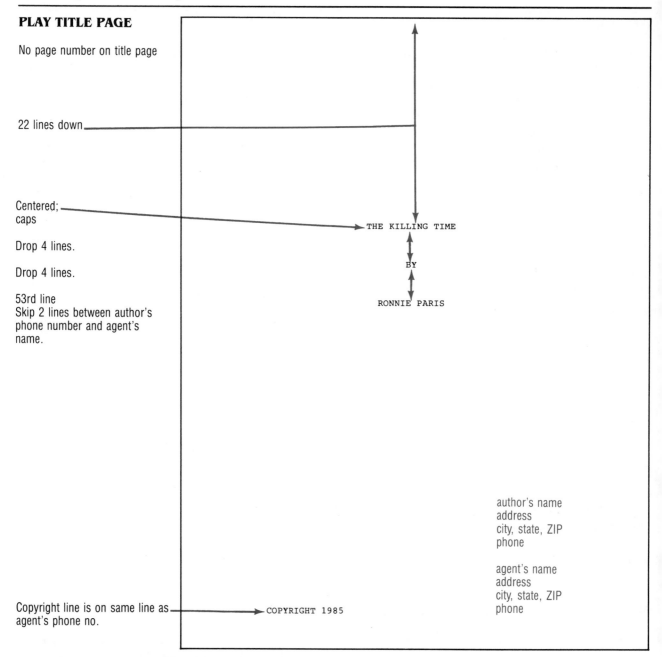

THE KILLING TIME

BY

RONNIE PARIS

author's name
address
city, state, ZIP
phone

agent's name
address
city, state, ZIP
phone

COPYRIGHT 1985

Most playwrights agree that it's a good idea to study the craft of playwriting. Consult your local university drama department for information, or write to the Dramatists Guild, 234 W. 44th Street, New York, NY, 10036, for information about recommended workshops.

Meanwhile, instead of discussing playwriting formats in abstract, let's look at a real title page, setting page, cast page, and scene.

Presenting—*The Killing Time.*

Curtain going up!

SETTING: BACK OF WARSAW'S MILLINERY, THE WORKROOM, STAGE LEFT
                                  AND A SMALL SECTION, STAGE RIGHT, BACKYARD.

                                  UPSTAGE WALL OF WORKROOM, STAGE RIGHT, HAS A PLACE
                                  FOR HANGING COATS, APRONS, ETC. FOR PEOPLE WHO WORK
                                  IN SHOP, SHELF ABOVE RACK.

                                  UPSTAGE WALL OF WORKROOM, CENTER, FILLED WITH ROWS
                                  OF WOODEN SHELVES FOR BOXES, WOODEN DOWELS TO HANG
                                  HALF-FINISHED HATS, VARIOUS MILLINERY SUPPLIES: RIBBONS,
                                  THREADS, FEATHERS, BUCRIM, NEEDLES, ETC.

                                  UPSTAGE RIGHT WALL OF WORKROOM, DOOR LEADING TO
                                  BATHROOM.

                                  CENTER RIGHT WALL OF WORKROOM, A SCREEN DOOR LEADING
                                  TO BACKYARD.

                                  DOWNSTAGE OF SCREEN DOOR, WALL CONTAINS MORE
                                  SHELVES HOLDING RECORD COLLECTION, PLAYER, JARS OF
                                  PICKLES, OLD ORDERS, FELT BODIES. HARRY'S ZITHER HANGS
                                  ON WALL ABOVE SHELVES.

                                  LEFT WALL OF SHOP IS CURTAINED OFF, CENTER, ENTRANCE TO
                                  STOCK ROOM, OFFSTAGE. AS CURTAIN IS PULLED ASIDE, WE
                                  CAN SEE WALL OF FINISHED HATS HANGING ON WOODEN DOW-
                                  ELS. THE 'FRONT' OF THE SHOP, OFFSTAGE, PAST STOCKROOM.

                                  DOWNSTAGE LEFT IS A STEAM TABLE OPERATED BY A FOOT
                                  PEDAL. SHELVES ABOVE TABLE CONTAIN WOODEN BLOCKS FOR
                                  SHAPING HATS, STOCK OF FELT BODIES IN LARGE GREY CARD-
                                  BOARD BOXES, HALF FINISHED ORDERS HANG ON WOODEN
                                  DOWELS.

                                  A WASHLINE EXTENDS FROM UPSTAIRS LANDING TO OFFSTAGE
                                  RIGHT, BRANCHES OF A TREE.

CAST:
HARRY WARSAW. . . . . .AGED 39 AT BEGINNING OF PLAY.
PAULA WARSAW, HIS WIFE. . . . . .ABOUT THE SAME AGE.
LENNY WARSAW, THEIR SON . . . . .ABOUT FIFTEEN WHEN THE PLAY OPENS.
BARBARY WARSAW, DAUGHTER . . . . .AGED 8, 14 AND 30.
MARY HOWARD, SEAMSTRESS, BLACK, MID 20'S.
MRS. BOWEN, SALESWOMAN, WASP, SLIGHT LIMP, LATE 50'S.
ROMEO SANTINI, MILLINERY SUPPLY SALESMAN, LATE 20'S.

TIME:
LATE 30'S, MID 40'S, EARLY 60'S.

ACT I:

LIGHTS UP ON READING STAND, STAGE RIGHT. AN AUDITORIUM, A PICTURE OF EISENHOWER, AN AMERICAN FLAG. BARBARA (30) ENTERS, CARRYING A BOOK, WHICH SHE PLACES ON STAND, LOOKS AT AUDIENCE FOR A MOMENT, WAITS FOR THEM TO 'SETTLE DOWN,' BEGINS:

BARBARA (30)

I'd like to welcome you to tonight's poetry reading.
(PAUSE)
Before I begin, I've been asked to say a few words about the sources of my poetry.
(PAUSE)
Invariably, I am asked, 'How long does it take to write a poem?' A poem can take a moment, an hour . . . or as in the case of tonight's poem? A lifetime.
(PAUSE)
I'm asked if I 'know' my poem before I write it.
(SHAKES HER HEAD, SMILES)
Always, my poem knows more than I do. I write to discover what I do not know.
(PAUSE)
Where do I get my inspiration from? Is the poem I've written taken from my 'real' life? The sources are as varied as the world in which I live. All I see and feel is my 'real' life . . .
(PAUSE, SMILES)
. . . so is all that I imagine.
(PAUSE)
And . . . while it may be true . . . as some of my students seem to think, that God arrives in the middle of the night and touches me, it is equally true that he simply refuses to do so unless he catches me hard at work.
(PAUSE, BACKGROUND SOFTLY,

HARRY'S VOICE, ARIA)

Too bad God is the inspiration and not the paymaster . . . for poets rarely get rich. They sing. It's a rare disease, this writing poetry, not curable.
(SOUND RISES)
Often a poem appears in a dream. The poem I'm going to read to you appeared in just such a manner. It flew in like a barn swallow, swooping and diving, puling away and returning. I tried chasing it . . . I longed for sleep. The bird refused to build a nest elsewhere; I knew a poem was about to be born. I couldn't deny hearing it or resist giving it a home. It arrived in techni-color, accompanied by music . . .
(SOUND UP HARRY, VESTI LA GUIBBA, FULL)
I call it THE KILLING TIME.
(BEGINS TO READ FROM HER TEXT)
I had a dream last night.
I dreamt I was three people,
I kept running . . . running.
I couldn't find us.
(LIGHTS BEGIN TO FADE ON BARBARA (30) AS SHE CROSSES TO DOLLHOUSE STAGE RIGHT, STANDS, LOOKING DOWN AT IT.)

BARBARA (8, OFFSTAGE VOICE)

This is the house my father built. It's perfect. Each piece of furniture is carved by hand. The old fashioned kitchen has a fireplace. On winter evenings we roast marshmallows, sit around drinking apple cider and telling stories. My family is just the right number . . . four.
(AS BARBARA (30) REACHES DOWN, PICKING UP DOLL FIGURES)
Mother . . . father . . . Lenny, the boy . . . the girl . . . me.

LENNY ENTERS FROM ABOVE STAIRS, RUNS THROUGH SCREEN DOOR INTO BACK OF THE STORE.

HARRY, AT WORK AT STEAMTABLE, STOPS, CROSSES TO REGISTER, GIVES LENNY MONEY, HANDS HIM LARGE GREY HATBOX.

LENNY EXITS THROUGH CURTAIN, STAGE LEFT.

A BEAT, BARBARA (8) WEARING BLUE VELVET POLISH COSTUME, DASHES DOWNSTAIRS, ACROSS BACKYARD, INTO BACK OF STORE.

BARBARA (8)

Daddy! Daddy! Look at me! Look at me!
(RUNS TO HARRY)
Look what Mommy made!

SANTINI ENTERS, SETS DOWN SUITCASE WITH SAMPLES.

SANTINI

Ciao!

HARRY

Look who's here . . .

PART 4

Mail Call

This section will cover everything you need to know to perform one of the most important acts in your career as a writer: getting your manuscript to the publisher! (Mailing information for Photography can be found under Photography in Et Cetera.)

All information necessary to move your book, article, script, or short story will be discussed on the following pages. These include:

MAILING INFORMATION—a general overview of the United States Post Office's mail services.

THE COVER UPS—envelopes, wrappers, and boxes. Also included is a handy checklist for making sure your manuscript is prepared correctly for mailing.

POSTAGE GUIDE—information on post office and private carriers, postage rates, AT-A-GLANCE POSTAGE GUIDE, and Mailing Checklist.

MAILING INFORMATION

The United States Postal Service is the major carrier of mail in this country. In spite of occasional criticisms of the service, they do a remarkable job moving millions of pieces of mail every day. Although most of the regular mail does get through safely and on time, it's a good idea to use either certified or registered mail to help ensure safe, prompt delivery. These services provide a record of when and to whom mail was sent and when it was delivered. Requesting a signed return receipt also indicates who accepted it. And, of course, registered or certified mail does get the attention of the recipient. Considering the huge amounts of mail that come into a publishing house, it can't hurt to have your material stand out from the rest.

The post office also has expedited delivery or priority mail services available. Essentially, these serve to alert the mail movers to keep the pieces moving, not to toss them on a pile where they may remain for several hours. Don't be penny foolish. Although it's much cheaper to send something Fourth Class or even book rate, you lose precious time while saving relatively little money. Send material First Class whenever possible. Not only will your mail not be delayed, it's more likely to be in better condition when it arrives. The main reason First Class costs more is that it gets to where it's supposed to go first. It doesn't lie around in bags or on shelves getting battered by all that extra handling while waiting for space with the next available carrier.

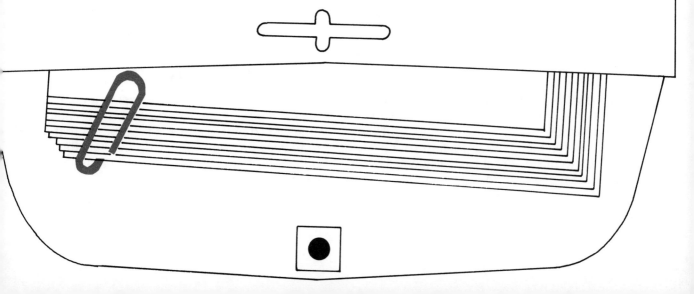

Sending material first class also raises your GII (Good Impression Index). It means you think enough of your work to spend the extra money for top-flight postal accommodations for your package.

The post office also has an overnight delivery system. The extra expense could be cost-effective if you're sending off material that needs to be seen quickly.

There are private mail carriers used mostly by business people who want delivery at a specified time. They're more expensive than the post office's similar services. The added cost may be justified if the service has a reputation for on-time, guaranteed delivery.

For specific information regarding the mailing of photographs, graphics, or other bulky material, check the Photography mailing tips in Et Cetera (pages 175-76).

THE COVER-UPS

You could fit a cover letter, relatively short proposal (about three pages), CV, and stamped, self-addressed envelope in a regular business-size envelope by pushing down as hard as you could to make the flattest package possible. However, you'd have a neater package, and less chance of having it go through transit gaping open, if you folded everything over just once and put it into a larger envelope, such as a 9½"x6". If your material is bulkier, it should be sent flat in a 9"x11" or larger envelope.

Complete book manuscripts can be sent in stationery boxes or wrapped in heavy paper stiffened with sheets of cardboard atop and under the manuscript. Many people enclose these wrapped manuscripts in book bags, those large mailing envelopes with plastic bubble liners, which help protect the packages during transit.

All addresses should be legible and accurate. For relatively little money, you can have labels prepared with your return address on them. Also, make sure that all directions to the mail handler are included on the envelope or wrapper. Even when using full-rate services, stamp your package First Class to make sure it isn't accidentally thrown into a pile of third-class material.

With international mailings, you run into some situations that require a little extra effort to assure safe, prompt delivery:

Make sure you know what the proper postage is for the country of destination. The best way to find out is to check with the post office. The fees may have changed between the time you sat down to write your proposal and the moment when you took it out of the typewriter.

Wrap your material in strong envelopes or coverings. Make sure the address contains everything needed for delivery. Some foreign countries write the city first and then the street, for example. Many—such as Great Britain and Canada—add six-figure directional codes, much like American zip codes, that must be used to assure efficient delivery. You may also have to indicate the contents of a package on a label to be affixed to the wrapper to satisfy customs requirements.

Send a self-addressed envelope for material you want returned. But *don't send American postage with it.* The stamps would be of value only to a collector. Instead, enclose International Reply Coupons, which you can buy at the post office.

Make sure your work doesn't sail through the Dire Straits on a slow freighter. Use AIR MAIL/PAR AVION markers to alert postal workers to put the mail on a plane.

Note: Make sure you keep accurate records reflecting:

a. The name of the publication and the person to whom you sent a submission;

b. The date the submission was sent;

c. How the submission was sent (Federal Express, registered mail, regular mail, etc.);

d. Date of first response;

e. Nature of response (accepted/rejected/request for further discussion, etc.);

f. Date of return of material (if applicable).

RATES AND WEIGHTS

We recommend that you invest in a good-quality postal scale—one that goes up to a reading of at least two pounds. Check for a brand that offers to replace the removable strip that has the rates printed on it with an updated strip if the rates change.

PREPARING THE MANUSCRIPT FOR MAILING—DO'S AND DON'TS

- Don't punch holes in it.
- Don't put it into a loose-leaf binder.
- Don't fold it.
- Don't staple it.
- Do read it over again to check for typos and missing pages.
- Do check to see that all needed enclosures are accounted for.
- Do make certain you've included necessary return postage and self-addressed envelopes. (You may also want to enclose a self-addressed label.)
- Do enclose a self-addressed reply postcard.
- Do recheck your cover letter. (See sample cover letters in appropriate sections.)
- Do put the manuscript in a secure box. A typing paper box is best. If you usually use computer printout paper and don't have an empty typing-paper box, you can buy secure boxes at the post office. Put your name and the addressee's name on the box. Tape or tie it with string or strong rubber bands so it won't open en route. Wrap the box in strong craft paper with your name and the addressee's name on the paper.

POSTAGE CHART FOR LARGER MANUSCRIPTS

Weight in Ounces	9x12 Envelope includes 9x12 SASE** plus no. of pages	9x12 SASE** (for return) plus no. of pages	First-Class Rate (check your local post office)
less than 2		1 to 2	_____
2	1 to 4	3 to 8	_____
3	5 to 10	9 to 12	_____
4	11 to 16	13 to 19	_____
5	17 to 21	20 to 25	_____
6	22 to 27	26 to 30	_____
7	28 to 32	31 to 35	_____
8	33 to 38	36 to 41	_____
9	39 to 44	42 to 46	_____
10	45 to 49	47 to 52	_____
11	50 to 55	53 to 57	_____
12	56 to 61	58 to 63	_____

Any first-class package weighing over twelve ounces is assessed by geographical zones, as is any fourth-class package regardless of weight.

1. Even if the weight is low, the postage charge is higher for oversized mail; in this case, the material was being sent in a 9x12 envelope instead of a #10.

2. Incidentally, the authors suggest using a larger envelope, since it means fewer folds for the manuscript—and fewer folds makes the manuscript easier for an editor to handle.

3. For return postage on an SASE to be mailed in Canada or any other country outside of the United States, enclose International Reply Coupons (also called IRC), which are available at most post offices. If yours doesn't carry any, you can order them or you can enclose a personal check for the amount of return postage, although some publishers do not like the added responsibility of recording and cashing checks.

MAILING CHECKLIST
Enclosures

Manuscript—Pages in correct sequence ☐

Cover letter—Name spelled correctly ☐
        Address checked ☐
        Relevant information included in
        letter ☐

Return, self-addressed post card to acknowledge receipt of mailed material (optional) ☐

Mailing envelope, stamps, and cardboard back-
ing for return of material ☐

Photographs or other art (if relevant);
see pages 175-76 ☐

Releases, permissions, clearances (if relevant) ☐

MAILING DETAILS

Book Bag ☐
Box ☐
Bubble Envelope ☐

First Class ☐
Certified ☐
Registered ☐
Express (U.S. Postal Service) ☐

PRIVATE COURIER SERVICE
Name: _____
Delivery No.: _____

Date Sent: _____
Cost: _____

Acknowledgment Received:
Date: _____
How (Phone, Card, Letter): _____
From whom: _____
Material Returned: yes ☐   no ☐

Et Cetera

This section is a treasure trove of information, checklists, logs, worksheets, and document samples that you'll find invaluable, and that you'll consult many times during your writing career.

The following is a list of some of these important writers' aids, along with a brief description of their function.

Agents

What agents do, and how and where to find an agent. Plus: sample letter requesting representation.

Special Letters for Special Needs

Included are samples of letters needed—(1) to advise the publisher about details (such as corrections or deletions) before your book is printed; (2) to request that the book's rights revert to you and that you be allowed to purchase the plates or film to reprint it; (3) to contact other publishers for resale of the book.

Also included are two sample permissions letters: (1) requesting permission to quote material in your book; (2) requesting permission to reproduce illustrations, graphs, or charts.

Correcting Typewritten Copy

All you ever needed to know about correcting typos so no one will ever know there was a typo there!

The Proofing Process

Tips on how to use computer "spell check" programs, plus a complete At-a-Glance guide to proofreading; also, proofreading symbols, and how to use them in galley proofs and text.

At-a-Glance Guides

Two other At-a-Glance guides are included: one for your typist, which will assure that your manuscript will be typed exactly as you want it pre-

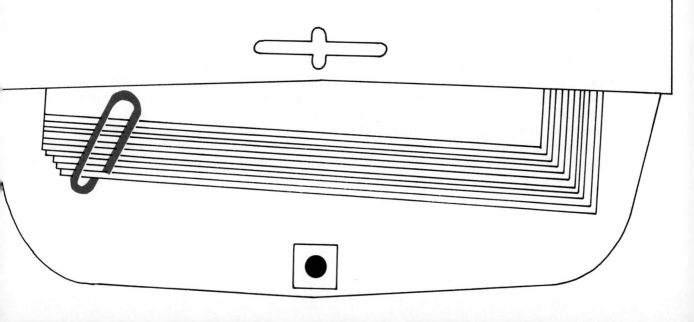

pared. (And if you're your own typist, the guide will make sure you don't forget what to do!) The other is an At-a-Glance guide to footnotes, illustrations, and captions that will be especially helpful to you if you submit to journals or write research reports.

Special Tips for Photographers

Information and checklists that will help you handle photo submissions wisely.

Checklists and Worksheets

Includes an Editorial Checklist, providing a means of keeping track of dates, content, deadlines, style, and writing mechanics for articles and stories. The Book Progress Checklist provides an easy-to-use means of keeping track of chapters as they are being written; and also provides a way for you to keep track of front matter (e.g., title page, epigraph, personal biography, lists of tables, lists of captions) and back matter (e.g., chapter notes, footnotes, appendices). In addition, there is an easy-to-use work progress list for keeping track of the final stages of the work, including checking page numbers, correcting errors in final copy, and securing needed releases; an editorial correspondence checklist tracking when and to whom correspondence was sent; a research correspondence log providing a record of

contacts, dates of contact, nature of research, and replies; and a book proposal worksheet that will help you think through the process of preparing a proposal.

Logs

- Telephone Expense Log—Provides an easy-to-keep record of telephone calls for each project, including date, time, person called, project, and comments. (This is especially valuable for tax records.)
- Frequent Contact Sheet—Provides a complete record of the contacts made with a publisher and/or editor while doing a book or article.
- Submission Log for Nonfiction Books—Provides a record of books submitted, date and means of submission, acceptance or rejection dates, comments, and rights sold.
- Submission Log for Magazines (Fiction and Nonfiction)—Provides a record of stories and articles submitted, date and means of submission, acceptance or rejection dates, comments, and rights sold.

The Writer's Special Bill of Rights

Key points on copyright that writers need to know to protect their interests in their works. Also included: copyright log to keep track of registered material.

AGENTS

An agent acts in behalf of someone. For writers, this usually means the agent presents a book or a script (usually in the form of a proposal) to a potential buyer and bargains for the best deal between the principals. Although authors can sell their own work and make their own deals, there are situations in which only agents can present ideas: with minor exceptions, this is true for screenplays and TV productions. (Producers find

this helps avoid plagiarism charges from writers who say their work has been used without credit or payment. By restricting submissions to agents, producers have a bona fide record of when, and from whom, they saw and accepted or rejected material.)

Agents work on a commission fee dependent on a percentage of what they earn for their clients from a publisher or producer.

Agents can pursue a sale on your behalf, leaving you free to work on other projects. Because they know the market, they can aim their efforts toward editors most likely to respond quickly (and, one hopes, positively). They also understand the terms regarding rights in a contract and can make sure you get to keep those you should have and get the best deal for those you sell. (*Negotiating Your Rights*, a pamphlet published by the Council of Writers Organizations, offers an overview of writers' rights from many top agents. The pamphlet is available for $5.50 sent to Holly Redell, Executive Director, CWO, 12H, 160 West End Ave., New York, NY 10023.)

Where to Find an Agent

Writers often get their agents through other writers. New writers can contact agents in other ways.

Writer's Market and *Fiction Writer's Market* provide lists of agents, along with information on how they prefer to be contacted. Some prefer recommendations; some will accept direct requests for representation. These publications also cite agents who specialize in placing certain types of books. *Literary Market Place* (LMP) also lists agents.

You can also check with the Society of Author's Representatives (SAR) and the Independent Literary Agents Association (ILAA). Current addresses for these organizations can be found in *WM* and *FWM*.

You can also meet agents at conferences given by national writers' groups, such as the American Society of Journalists & Authors, Science Fiction Writers of America, and many others. Newspapers sometimes run announcements about such conferences. An invaluable source of information is the May issue of *Writer's Digest*, which carries a complete list of writers' conferences in all states for the year.

For a list of literary and theatrical agencies, you can consult Writers Guild, West. One part of the list indicates agencies that will consider material from new writers. (WG, West, 8955 Beverly Blvd., Los Angeles, CA 90048.)

Should you pay an agent to read your manuscript? Some agents do charge what they call a reading or pre-publication fee. This is usually a set fee (not a commission) that can run anywhere from a minimal charge to several hundred dollars.

If you choose to pay an agent for reading your manuscript, know what you're getting for the money. Some agents will make general observations; others will be more specific regarding suggestions that might make the manuscript more saleable. In any event, keep in mind that you may not be able to sell the manuscript even after making the suggested revisions.

Making the First Move

When you've decided to approach an agent and ask to be represented, do the following:

1. Prepare a letter requesting representation (sample follows).

2. Have clippings of your published work ready to send on.

3. Prepare a fully detailed proposal of your book idea, and be ready to send it along if requested in the agent's return letter.

4. A new author should have the book manuscript finished, or as close to completion as possible, so that it can be sent on if requested.

Once you've sent the letter off, relax. Don't expect an immediate reply. At least a month, sometimes more, may pass before you get an answer. Meanwhile, spend that waiting time polishing your manuscript. Get that proposal or outline in better shape. Make sure the chapters you may be sending on are of publishable quality.

Keep in mind the cardinal rule: Do not bug the agent for a reply—unless you want to enhance the chance that it will be a negative one.

For an expanded discussion of literary agents and their role, see *Literary Agents*, by Michael Larsen (Writer's Digest Books).

SAMPLE—Letter to agent requesting representation

Letterhead
Single-spaced
Block form

Margins, 1-1½″ all around

Cite reason for letter.

Referral (if relevant)

Describe book and your work in progress.

Your background

Your writing credits (if relevant)

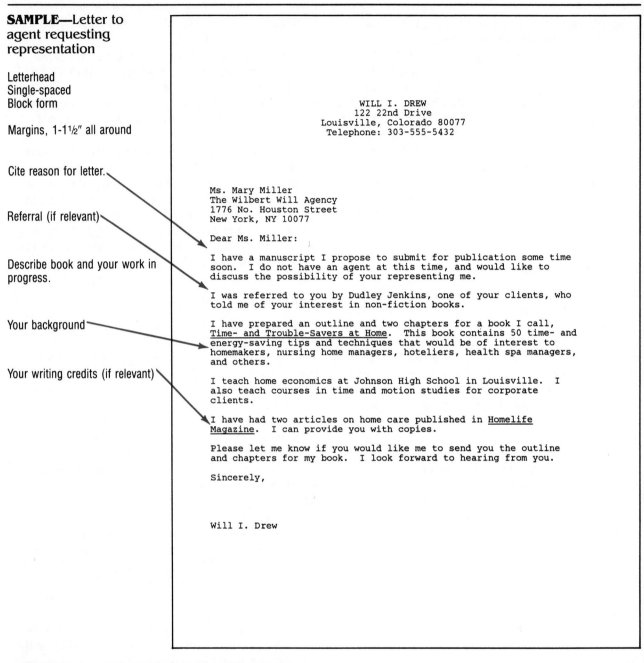

```
                            WILL I. DREW
                            122 22nd Drive
                       Louisville, Colorado 80077
                         Telephone: 303-555-5432


          Ms. Mary Miller
          The Wilbert Will Agency
          1776 No. Houston Street
          New York, NY 10077

          Dear Ms. Miller:

          I have a manuscript I propose to submit for publication some time
          soon.  I do not have an agent at this time, and would like to
          discuss the possibility of your representing me.

          I was referred to you by Dudley Jenkins, one of your clients, who
          told me of your interest in non-fiction books.

          I have prepared an outline and two chapters for a book I call,
          Time- and Trouble-Savers at Home.  This book contains 50 time- and
          energy-saving tips and techniques that would be of interest to
          homemakers, nursing home managers, hoteliers, health spa managers,
          and others.

          I teach home economics at Johnson High School in Louisville.  I
          also teach courses in time and motion studies for corporate
          clients.

          I have had two articles on home care published in Homelife
          Magazine.  I can provide you with copies.

          Please let me know if you would like me to send you the outline
          and chapters for my book.  I look forward to hearing from you.

          Sincerely,



          Will I. Drew
```

SPECIAL LETTERS FOR SPECIAL NEEDS

There are times in the life of a writer or author when certain situations develop that require specific responses. In this section, you'll find samples of letters to write for such situations as:

- The Reprinting of Your Edition: How to advise the publisher about corrections, updates, deletions, and other changes that need to be made.
- Your Book is Going Out of Print: How to request the rights to the book and acquire the film that you may be able to resell to another publishing company.
- After the Rights Have Reverted to You: How to contact other publishers who may be interested in buying the book.
- Reprint Package Letter
- Letter requesting permission to quote

SAMPLE MEMO—
Reprint corrections

(Letterhead is OK)

January 8, 1989

TO: Timothy Charles, Reprint Editor ———————— Name and address
         Lechat Publishing Company

FROM: Selena Thorne ———————— Name of editor
         333 1/2 13th Avenue
         New York, NY 12222

                    CORRECTIONS FOR REPRINT ————— Title of book

My book, The Cat's Meow: A Study in Communication, is to be ———— Title for memorandum

reprinted. I have noted the following corrections of proofs for ———— Page number each correction

the reprint: List all corrections.

1) After the word --Manx--add--and other breeds, including--
   page 2

2) Delete the last sentence of the first paragraph.--page 15

3) At bottom, add sentence--This has been affirmed by data.--
   page 22

                    _____   Sign it.

                    Selena Thorne   Keep copy on file.

● Letter requesting permission to reproduce illustrations, graphs, or charts
  All of the form letters shown here provide
guides for your own needs. Follow them, and they
may lead to a successful "afterlife" for your book.

SAMPLE LETTER—
Requesting rights to
book going out of print

Your name/address

Send registered mail

Request for reversion of rights

Mention clause in contract

Block business format

Title of book

Date of publication

Check contract

Type name

Signature

```
                              Your name here
                              Your address
                          Your town, state, ZIP




            Date




            Name of Editor
            Publishing House
            Address
            City, State, ZIP

            Dear_____

            According to clause number_____ of my contract for my book
            titled_____
            dated:_____, rights to the book will revert to me
            upon written request.

            This letter constitutes a request for rights to revert to me.

            As stipulated in the contract, I look forward to hearing from you
            within_____days.

            Sincerely,



            Your name
```

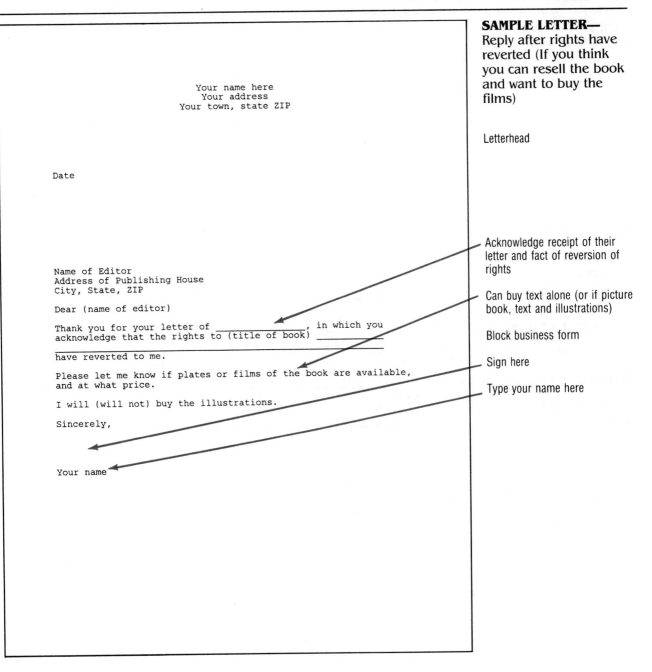

SAMPLE LETTER—
Reply after rights have reverted (If you think you can resell the book and want to buy the films)

Letterhead

Acknowledge receipt of their letter and fact of reversion of rights

Can buy text alone (or if picture book, text and illustrations)

Block business form

Sign here

Type your name here

Letter content:

```
                    Your name here
                    Your address
                 Your town, state ZIP




     Date




     Name of Editor
     Address of Publishing House
     City, State, ZIP

     Dear (name of editor)

     Thank you for your letter of _____, in which you
     acknowledge that the rights to (title of book) _____

     have reverted to me.

     Please let me know if plates or films of the book are available,
     and at what price.

     I will (will not) buy the illustrations.

     Sincerely,



     Your name
```

SAMPLE LETTER—
for resale of book

Cover letter to publisher

Brief pitch

Enclose résumé.

Need a copy of manuscript

Copy of finished book

Copies of key reviews

If illustrated—résumé of illustrator

Enclose SASE.

Your name

```
                        Your name here
                        Your address
                     Your town, state, ZIP




        Date

        Name of Editor
        Publishing House
        Address
        City, State, ZIP

        Dear (name of editor):

        I am the author of (title of book)_____,
        published by_____in (date) _____.
        The rights to the book have reverted to me and [if relevant] to
        my illustrator, _____.

        The book was very successful in _____market.  It
        is a good book for your list because _____
        _____.  The audience for this
        book is _____
        _____.

        I enclose a resume of my work, some key reviews and comments on this
        book, a resume of the illustrator [if relevant], and a copy of the book.
        Please let me know if you would like to see a copy of the original
        manuscript.

        I look forward to hearing from you on this matter.

        Sincerely,



        Your name

        Encls.: book, resume, reviews, SASE
```

SAMPLE FORM LETTER—Requesting permission to quote from books or journal articles

Styles will vary in requesting permission. This is one example.

```
                        Your Letterhead


Date

Name of Publisher
Address
City, State, ZIP

Dear_____:

I would like to have permission to quote the following material:
"_____

_____

_____"

from (if a book, insert Title, Edition, and Year)
     (if a journal, insert Name of journal and article,
      Vol. No., page, and year)
by_____, in a book I am writing

under the title of_____,

to be published by _____, (address)_____


_____

for international distribution.  This request shall include all
future editions in all languages.

Credit to the original source of publication will be properly
given in a footnote following the quotation.

If permission of the author is also necessary, please provide me
with his/her address.  I enclose a stamped, self-addressed
envelope for your use.

                    Sincerely,


                    (Signature)_____
            Name and address_____
                              _____

PLEASE USE RELEASE FORM BELOW
_____
Permission to quote is granted on the terms stated in this letter.

Date _____      Name_____
                              Title _____
                              Company
                              Address_____
```

FORM LETTER—
Requesting permission
to reproduce
illustrations, graphs, or
charts

Styles will vary in requesting
permission. This is one
example.

Date

Name of Publisher
Address
City, State, ZIP

Dear_____:

I would like to have your permission to reproduce the following figure(s):

FIG. NO.   PAGE

_____   ____

_____   ____

from (if a book, insert title, edition, and year)
     (if a journal, insert name of journal and article, vol. no.,
     page, and year)

by _____, in a book I am

writing under the title of_____,

to be published by_____

(address)_____.

This request shall include all future editions in all languages.
Credit to the original source will be included in the legend(s).
If permission from the author is also necessary, please provide me with
his/her address so that I may request his/her permission, as well as the use
of the original illustration copy.

                              Sincerely,

                              Signature_____

                              Name_____
                              Address_____
                              City_____State_____ZIP_____

PLEASE USE RELEASE FORM BELOW

Permission is granted on the terms stated in this letter.

Date_____   Name _____

Title _____   Company _____

Address _____

CORRECTING TYPEWRITTEN COPY

One of the most difficult choices writers sometimes have to face is not which word to use or what the rules of grammar are in a particular case. Instead, it's how to make a correction on copy so that it doesn't look corrected.

With a computer, the correction can be made quickly and easily. The offending word, sentence, passage, etc., is located, changed on the disk, and saved in memory; then a new hard copy is printed out.

With a correcting ribbon in a typewriter, a correction can be made immediately by typing over the problem area with the special ribbon and retyping the corrected copy.

You can also make professional corrections when your page is out of the typewriter. Learn the skill of reinserting paper so that it lines up in precisely the same position it had been in previously (see explanation below). Then you can use the correcting ribbon and retype.

If you have no correcting ribbon, you can erase—very carefully—using a soft eraser that won't leave telltale signs behind. You can then reinsert the sheet into the typewriter and retype the correction.

Correcting fluid—or white out—can also be used on the mistakes. When you apply it to a page that is still in the typewriter, let it dry and then retype. If the page has been removed, apply the White Out, let it dry, and reinsert for the corrected version.

It takes practice to reinsert a sheet of paper so that it lines up in the right position. Professional typists know how to do this. Most writers don't but should. Briefly, it's done by reinserting the sheet and then releasing the platen so that you can move it around on the roller. Set the sheet so that the new typewritten letter, word, or line will appear in the space left by the deleted word material. Line up a vertical letter (an "i" or an "l") with the vertical line found in the center of the plastic indicator above the ribbon, or in some typewriters, above the daisywheel or ball element.

Another correction device is a chemically coated material placed over the mistake while the page is still in the typewriter. When the mistake is typed over, a tiny bit of white dust remains behind to hide the error. The correct letters are then typed over the now-hidden mistakes.

THE PROOFING PROCESS—NO ONE'S PREFECT. AND AND WE CAN PROVE IT.

The proofreading process is one of the most important elements in the production of a quality work. Professional proofreaders know how to search out more than spelling, grammar, and typos. They also know how to recognize style problems.

Before your manuscript is sent out, you should have done as exhaustive a proofreading job as possible on your own work. Check for spelling errors. (A note of caution to those computer users who have Spell Check or similar functions: Don't rely on your word processor to catch all your errors. For example, if you have a sentence that reads *He was form a far away country,* your program will pass it because it recognizes the word *form* as correct as it stands, although you meant to write: *He was* from *another country.*

Don't scan your copy; read it carefully to catch words you may have used too often or run-on sentences.

You may have to give your manuscript to someone else to type. Using the right editing symbols cuts down on typing errors caused by misinterpretations. (And you'll go up on your typist's Good Impression Index as well.)

Galley Proofs: Knowing how to use proofreading symbols can make it easier for you to proofread your proofs or galleys when they're sent back to you before your book or article is published. (And that's another reason you want to turn in a manuscript that's as close to being error-free as possible: a.e.'s [author's errors] can be charged against your advance while p.e.'s [printer's errors] are not charged for.) Article proofs are not usually sent back unless editorial changes were made in your copy or agreed to in advance.

Whether it's a matter of being right on a fact, or a point of grammar, don't let someone else catch you on an error that you might have prevented with a little effort. A motto that should be part of your work pattern is:

When in doubt, check it out.

An At-a-Glance Guide to proofreading follows.

AT-A-GLANCE GUIDE TO PROOFREADING

Corrections

Proposal, query, or cover letter

For that important first letter to an editor you must produce clean copy. It is unprofessional to send a proposal, query, or cover letter with extensive or obvious erasures, crossing out, or strikeovers.

Correction fluid is acceptable if you can produce clear copy. Correction tape is useful if you intend to send a clear, well-produced photocopy for multiple submission.

Final *accepted* article or book ms

Employ these most commonly used Proofreader's Correction Marks in final manuscript

Also: see full page of proofreader's symbols, page 166.

Paragraphing ⁋

Change words

Delete words ℓ

Add words ∧

Transpose letters ∩ *or* trs

Separate words/letters /

Close up words ⊂

Change Capital to lower case /ℓc

Change lower case to capital *cap* =

Indicate *italics* (any time you underline for emphasis it will be printed as italics)

Reverse sentences or paragraphs *rvs*

CORRECTING *FINAL* COPY WITH PROOFREADER'S MARKS

Paragraphing

Indicate a new paragraph with the symbol ⁋ before the word that is to begin the new paragraph.

Change Words

Cross through words and *rewrite above them,* either on the typewriter or by hand, in pencil or pen.

that
~~which~~

Jim
~~John~~

we
~~I~~

Delete Words

Indicate a deletion by a vertical or diagonal line through the letter, word, or words to be eliminated.

Indicate ~~one or more~~ deletions

Add Words

Add words *above* the line with a caret (∧) inserted below the line at the exact place of the addition.

told
The bus driver∧her the fare

to be
had∧paid in coins.

Transpose

Reverse letters/typos thus:

The bus driver told her the

faer had to be apid in coisn.

Separate Words

Separate run-together words with a vertical slash

Separate run-together words/with

a vertical/slash.

Close Up Words

Connect words to be closed up with a curved line

Connec t words to be clo sed up

with a cu rved line.

Change Capital to Lower Case

It was 9 A.M. *lc*

The Following Numbers are listed

as Numerals: *lc*

Change Lower Case to Capital

many manuscripts require notes.

D day was june 6. *cap*

Indicate Italics

Any underlining in your manuscript will be published as *italics.*

Reverse Sentences or Paragraphs

Whenever you wish to reverse the sequences of sentences or paragraphs, indicate it by using the letters *rvs.*

HOW TO USE PROOFREADING SYMBOLS

∧	Make correction indicated in margin
Stet	Retain crossed-out word or letter, let it stand (stet)
¶	Make a paragraph here
trs	Transpose words or letters
ℓ	Delete matter indicated (dele)
ℓ	Take out character indicated and close up
ℓ	Line drawn through a cap means lower case
⌒	Close up; no space
#	Insert a space here
Caps	Put in capitals
ital	Change to Italic
≡	Under letter or word means capital
—	Under letter or word means Italics
⌇	Under letter or word means boldface
⸴/	Insert comma
⩔ ⩔	Insert quotation marks

"Soap ∧love stories," said Douglas Marland stet, currently head writer of <u>As The World Turns</u> and formerly head writer of <u>general Hospital</u> Hospital and <u>Guiding Light</u> ∧and an actor and director, in his own right ∧are meant to make people feel the païns and the pässsions of the characters. They're also meaⁿt to make you thing about things the they do."

A GUIDE FOR YOUR TYPIST

Many writers find it's a good idea to let some-one else do the typing or word processing for them. If you're among those who see the wisdom in such a move, then you, and the person who will be working on your manuscript, will appreci-ate the following At-a-Glance Guide.

Use this to indicate directions to your typist or word-processor operator. In this way the chances for misinterpretation are greatly reduced, and the probability of producing more efficient and better looking copy is greatly increased.

AT-A-GLANCE MANUSCRIPT TYPIST'S GUIDE

Corrections	tape	☐
	cut in	☐
	liquid	☐
	strikeover	☐
Margins (in inches)	Top	_____
	Bottom	_____
	Left	_____
	Right	_____
Spacing of text	Single-space when	_____
	Double-space when	_____
	Triple-space when	_____
Remarks:		
Spacing in manuscript	Title to text	_____
	End of topic to subhead	_____
	Between title and subtitle	_____

Remarks:

Lines on each page   _____

Titles   All caps   ☐

                          Upper/lower case   ☐

                          Centered   ☐

                          Flush left   ☐

                          Indented _____ spaces

Chapter numbers   Roman   ☐

                          Arabic   ☐

Underline   Chapter titles   ☐

                          Subheads   ☐

                          Words   ☐

Remarks:

                          Phrases   ☐

Remarks:

                          Quotations   ☐

Remarks:

Page-number placement	Top ☐ Bottom ☐
	Left ☐
	Right ☐
	Center ☐
Boldface	Yes ☐
	No ☐

Remarks:

Check spelling with _____ Dictionary

(See attached list of frequent or unusual words.)

Hyphenate	Yes ☐
	No ☐

Remarks:

Justification	Yes ☐
	No ☐
Abbreviations	Standard ☐ Based on _____ Manual
	Special ☐ Based on _____ Manual

(See list of frequently used abbreviations.)

Quotations

Remarks on style:

AT-A-GLANCE GUIDE TO FOOTNOTES, ILLUSTRATIONS, AND CAPTIONS

Footnotes

Footnotes are comments at the bottom of a page. They give either your own comments or important facts, quotes, or opinions without interrupting the flow of your text. While such notes have an important place in research and technical papers and senior theses, if the fact is important, you should try to weave it in an interesting fashion into your manuscript.

Facts in footnotes

Book mention	Note the information the reader will need to locate the book.
Name of author	As on the title page, first name first. If two authors, each name is written first name first. Three authors: type the name of the first author, add *et al.,* the Latin abbreviation for *and others.*
Title of work	Underlined. If you use a subtitle, place a colon between the title and subtitle.
Facts of publication	*City* of publication; *date* of publication in parentheses. If you have no date, type *n.d.* If you have no publisher, type *n.p.*
	The specific *page* or *pages* of the source. Use the abbreviations *p.* for page, and *pp.* for pages.
Journal mention	Check publisher for style guidelines.
Author's name	The author's name and the title of article are given as they appear in print—type author's first name first.
Title of article	Place quotation marks around title of article.
Journal	Underline name of the journal (it will appear in italics).
Numbers	Current practice is Arabic numerals for volume and for page numbers. If you list the volume, you must then omit *p.* for *page.*
Placement	Type each footnote number and note in your drafts so that you will be able to gauge the space you need at the bottom of each page.
Numbering system	Use Arabic numbers in consecutive order through each chapter, or through entire manuscript. For example, if there are three notes on page one, the first footnote on page two is number 4.

Placement of numbers in text in footnote	Raise typewriter up half a line, place your number slightly above the line above the last punctuation of the sentence to be footnoted. See "Typing of footnote," below.
Bottom margin of page	In advance, mark your paper to allow a deep 1½" bottom margin. If you plan many footnotes, use a precut cardboard form. Mark each page with a nonreproducing blue pencil. You will also have to allow room between the text and the footnote.
Space between text and footnote	Allow three lines between last line of text and first footnote.
Typing of footnote	After space between text, indent as for a paragraph. Raise the carriage of the typewriter half a line and write the number. Do not use a period or a parenthesis. Lower the carriage (to the third line from the text), skip one space, and type the footnote in single-spacing.
If using word processor	Follow the special instructions of your software package for formatting, but unless specifically instructed, you can follow these general rules.
More than one line	If the note goes beyond one line, type runovers flush with left margin.
Space between footnotes	Double-space between each note.
More than one footnote following each other	Indent each note. Begin with raised number, skip a space. Capitalize first letters of names. Place a period after the name. End the entire note with a period.
To continue long note on next page	If you haven't gauged the space properly, in the absence of any special style rules of the publisher, continue your note at the bottom of the next page ahead of any notes on that page.

Book Illustrations

Types of illustrations	Illustrations, sometimes called *figures*, may consist of original illustrations or photographs,* various commercial artwork, reproductions, charts, diagrams, graphs, data, plans, maps, or other visual material.
Consult art director	Different publishers and periodicals take different style approaches to presentation, numbering, margins, captions, and mounting. Find out if illustrations will be placed near text, clustered, or at the end of the manuscript. Ask how captions and legends are to be attached to illustrations. For further information, read Frances W. Zweifel's *A Handbook of Biological Illustration*, Phoenix Press (Chicago: University of Chicago Press, 1961).

*For presentation of photographs, see page 175 in this checklist.

Presentation of each illustration	
Line and tone drawings	Consult your art director for specific instructions. Usually, the drawings are prepared for $1/3$ reduction, and are prepared with India ink on white, quality artboard.
Captions for drawings	Consult art director. Many guidelines request that labels and lead lines be positioned on a tissue overlay.
To reproduce your own graphs, charts, diagrams	Use special paper with nonreproduceable blue lines.
Mounting	If less than 8½"x11", mount on bond paper with no rag content with *dry-mounting tissue-paper adhesive.* (This is available in sheets or rolls from photographer's supply stores.) Do not use rubber cement.
How many on a page?	Each illustration is usually placed on a separate piece of paper; however, you can place two smaller illustrations two to a page. Either number and label separately or give each group a number or letter and an overall caption. Key to text!
Margins	Presentation requires at least *one inch* margins on all four sides. Wider margins are permissible.
Captions within margins?	Some publishers require that captions be contained within the margins. See your publisher's guidelines. Some publishers prefer for each caption (or legend) to be typed on 8½"x11" paper and double-spaced with one-inch margins. (Keep a copy of all the captions for your own records.)
Binders?	If publisher requests a binder for illustrations, before mounting, compensate for the binding by creating a wider margin at left. Also leave a wide margin at bottom of page.
Numbering or keying of figures	
Creating a unique keying system	Assign numbers, letters, or a combination of both. Be consistent. If there is only one type of illustration, number and key them in the order they will be found in the text.
If illustrations will be near text	If your charts, diagrams, graphs, illustrations, photographs, etc. are to be placed near relevant text, and there are several types of illustrations, label them all as *figures* (Figure 1., Figure 2., Figure 3.) *and number them consecutively.*
More of one type of illustration than others—or one type is more important	Give each type its own "label." Number as in a separate series. For example: Chart 1, Chart 2, Chart 3 or Graph 1, Graph 2, Graph 3, or Plan or Map or Diagram 1, 2, 3, 4, 5, 6, etc.

Frontispiece	Assign (but do not type in) a number to the frontispiece (the illustration that faces or immediately precedes title page).
If illustrations are to be placed at end of manuscript	Follow sequential manuscript pagination for all back-of-book illustrations.

Caption, Title, or Legend

The description of an illustration is called either a *caption,* a *title* or a *legend.* Often it is called a *legend.* These descriptions can be one or more sentences. They do not necessarily have to be complete sentences: short descriptions will do. KEEP A RECORD OF YOUR LEGENDS!

Be consistent	Use a consistent form of capitalization, numbering, and placement of underlining and punctuation.
Typing a legend	Publishers have different guidelines for typing of legends (captions, titles). Many request each legend be presented on a separate 8½"x11" page. In the absence of other instructions, following are standard guidelines:
	Indent as if in a paragraph.
Sample	**Fig. 13. Three members of the expedition carefully remove earth from the mosaic floor.**
	Type each legend as if it will be placed beneath each illustration.
	Center short captions.
	Use entire width of the illustration for longer caption, title, legend.
Marking or keying text	Mark text to show editor general or specific placement of each illustration. Check publisher's guidelines.
If lettered by hand	If you letter a caption by hand, use *black* drawing ink.
On the back of illustration	Show number, title, and location in text *lightly* (in pencil) on back of each illustration. Do not emboss the illustration.
Relationship of number placement to legend (or title or caption)	Generally, the number is placed first.
Sample	**Fig. 9. The Fort**
	Fig. 30. Erie Canal horses
Folding large illustrations	Consult a manual of illustration for information on folding larger-scale material, since it must be folded from right to left with no more than 7½ inches from the left side.
Placement of the number	Make sure the number of the folded material is *visible* by placing the number (centered) on an outward facing fold.

Permissions	Obtain *written permission* from the original publisher and author(s) for the use of all material. You must do so even from publishers of your own works.
	See sample permissions letter, page 161.
Illustrations from books and journals	Indicate in the margin of each letter the illustration number to which it refers.
Tables	For *tables*, obtain written permission from the original publisher and author(s) for the use of directly reproduced tabular material—even publishers of your own works. Include the complete source of publication in a footnote accompanying the table. Follow book/journal credit.
	Indicate on the margin of the permission letter the table number to which it refers.
Quotes	Include written permission for quotes with the pertinent chapter (or consult your editor for guidelines). Indicate in the margin of the letter the page number on which the quotation appears.
Credit line	A credit line should contain the following information:
	For a book—author or editor, title, edition, city in which publisher is located, year, publisher.
	For a journal—authors, title of article, journal abbreviation, volume, page, and year.
Illustration mailing procedures	Refer to publisher's guidelines for folding of larger items.
	Illustrations may be presented with the manuscript. List the illustrations in your cover letter. Keep a copy of the list and the captions.
	If you send/deliver the illustrations in a separate package or at a different time, enclose a cover letter with your name, address, phone, title of manuscript, and name of editor.
	Use protective backing in the package.
	Mark: *PHOTOGRAPHS: DO NOT BEND*
	Send by express mail, private courier, or messenger service.

SPECIAL TIPS FOR PHOTOGRAPHERS

Before Mailing: What to Write on Photographs

Slides (Wide Margin)
1. Subject Identification:
   If of scientific nature, make as accurate as possible
   If person, give name, location, other pertinent details
   If product, name of product, location of picture
   If place, give location—be specific
2. Your name, address, phone number

Slides (Narrow Margin)
1. Stock Number: your unique numbering system for quick retrieval
2. Copyright symbol: ©19____ (do not fill in until you send it) or use Roman Numerals— MCMLXXXVIII (1988)

Black-and-White
1. On back with rubber stamp, gummed label, or with felt-tip pen or grease pencil:

2. Your name, address, city, state, ZIP, and phone number
3. Your unique stock code number
4. Copyright symbol: ©19____ (do not fill in until you send it) or use Roman Numerals

Sample Rubber Stamp

Your Name _____
Address _____
City _____ State _____ ZIP ____
Agency (if you have one): _____
Subject: _____
Event: Football-Meadowlands _____
Date: March 22, 1987 _____
File No.: F/20/23 (3-22-87)* _____

*F = football file, 20 = number of rolls shot, picture is #23, date

Mailing Your Photographs

In Advance of Mailing
Design personal stationery for letters and invoices.

In presenting pictures, keep logical themes together.

Display or number the pictures in logical order of viewing.

Protect B&W photographs with *onion skin* paper separation.

Enclose a self-addressed post card to acknowledge receipt and possible interest.

Mark package: PHOTOGRAPHS—DO NOT BEND!

Slides (or transparencies): place in a large vinyl or cardboard sleeve. For additional protection, use individual holders (such as Kimac Protector—478 Long Hill Road, Guildford, CT 06437). Present large groups of sleeve-slides in a labeled, three-ring, loose-leaf book.

Mailers: use a stiff cardboard mailer (such as Calumet—Box 405, 16920 State Street, South Holland, IL 60475). Insert the Calumet package into a larger envelope to mail to your client. Or use a heavy manila envelope with cardboard stiffener, and enclose a stamped, self-addressed envelope big enough to hold the photographs. (Ten to twenty prints can fit in a 9"x12" manila envelope.)

Don'ts
B&W: Don't send *negatives;* send contact sheets or selected blowups.

Transparencies: Don't send originals; send duplicates only.

Don't handwrite your letters (it isn't businesslike).

How to Mail
First class
Certified mail (can be tracked if lost)
Express Mail or courier service (if requested and your fee includes it)

Creating a File Retrieval System for Photographs
Each system is entirely personal. You may want a number or an alphabet base, or a combination of

both. Some photographers prefer a 1-2-3 system for negatives, slides, prints. Example: 1. Negative, 2. Transparency, 3. Print. Or you can assign letters of the alphabet to areas of *specialty*. Codes can be anything you decide: C-Celebrities, T-TV personalities, S-Stage personalities, P-Political personalities, So-Soap Stars, etc.

You will need a simple number code for number of rolls shot (you number each roll), and the number of the frame you are presenting.

Keep a separate record of your copyrights. You can copyright a single photograph or a group of photographs (under one general heading).

PHOTOGRAPHY: SUBMISSION CHECKLIST

Personalized stationery ☐

Copyright: Single ☐   or group copyright ☐

Check: name of editor, address and ZIP ☐

Query letter (Send separate one for each request)
  Short request/guidelines
    Stock house ☐ Magazine ☐
  Personal letter asking for future assignments ☐
  Proposal for photo story idea ☐
  Asking for representation (agent) ☐
  Requesting permission to shoot·story on
    speculation ☐

Cover letter (Check pertinent item.)
  Submission on speculation ☐
  Submission in response to query ☐
  Submission on letter of agreement or contract ☐
  Selling of stock photographs (multiple
    submission) ☐

See page 175 for what (how) to write on photographs.

Details
  Does material relate to publication's needs? ☐
  Are enclosures identified and listed? ☐
  Did I list my publication credits? ☐
  Are the photographs labeled and captioned?* ☐
  Black and White (no negatives!)
    My name, address, city, state, ZIP, and phone ☐
    Code or file *number* of photograph ☐
    Accurate *caption:* Details, names, place ☐
    Cardboard mailer ☐
    Copyright symbol on each photograph ☐
  Transparencies (not originals!)
    Place in individual holder ☐
    Place series in sleeve ☐
    Code or stock number ☐
    My name, address, phone ☐
    Accurate caption: Name, place, theme, series ☐
    Copyright symbol on each transparency ☐

Did I enclose:
  Release form? ☐
  My stock list? ☐
  Stamped, Self-mailer for return of photographs? ☐
  Résumé (if needed)? ☐
  Publications or other credit list? ☐
  Post card (#1) acknowledging receipt of
    package? ☐
  Invoice (if photographs sold)? ☐
Mailed: First class ☐   Certified mail ☐
          Express Mail ☐   Other ☐ _____
Post card (#2) follow up request ☐

Did I record my submission? ☐
  What, where, to whom, date sent
  Code numbers for retrieval*
  Date and nature of response
  Date of follow up

SUBMISSION RECORD LOG: PHOTOGRAPHS

Photo code no. B&W Slides	How Mailed	Date	Topic or Description	Sent to: Contact, Phone	Magazine Ad Agency Other	Address	Comment	Date Ret'd.	Date Sold	Rights Sold	Fee

BOOK ILLUSTRATION: PRESENTATION CHECKLIST

IN ADVANCE

Check with editor and/or art director regarding illustrations expected. ☐

Check publisher's guidelines as to presentation and mounting of illustrations, and presentation of legends and captions. ☐

Check planned placement in book:
near text; ☐
grouped in center; ☐
grouped at end. ☐

Relate or key numbering system to placement in book. ☐

Should illustrations be divided in any way? _____
If so, how? _____

Should larger maps, plans, graphs, etc. be folded? _____

Should illustrations and/or photographs be returned? _____

I have asked ☐   I will ask ☐
_____ to return them.

I have made a complete list of numbered illustrations and pages. ☐

PRESENTATION DETAILS

Numbering
Is numbering style consistent (figures, letters or both)? ☐
If item is folded—is number on outside center? ☐
Does the legend, title, or caption *follow* the number? ☐
Did I indicate (or key) location in text? ☐

Captions
Separate page for each illustration or 8″x10″ photograph? ☐
Does the caption (title, legend) follow illustration number? ☐
Did I key location to text? ☐
Have I followed publisher's guidelines for attaching? ☐
Typing:
Did I indent first lines (as in a paragraph)? ☐
If short legend, did I center on page? ☐
Did I type the width of illustration? ☐
Hand-lettered: Did I use black drawing ink? ☐

Is caption writing style consistent?
Capitalization ☐
Punctuation ☐
Underlining ☐

Mounting
Outline traced ahead of time? ☐
No rag-content paper? ☐
Dry mounting tissue adhesive used? ☐
No rubber cement used? ☐
Two-to-a-page for smaller illustrations? ☐

Photographs
Arrow to indicate viewing direction? ☐
B&W: Did I check publisher's guidelines? ☐
Size:
8½″x11″—did I use *medium-weight* paper (no mounting needed)? ☐
smaller than 8½″x11″ ☐
Mounted: One to a page? ☐
Two to a page? ☐
Typewriter paper? ☐
Caption attached: yes ☐   no ☐
Finish: matte ☐   glossy ☐
Transparencies:
Submitted in sleeve? ☐
Additional protector? ☐

Permissions
Submitted _____ release forms
Need _____ (for entire book)
Submitted _____ copies permissions letters
Need _____ (for entire book)
Letters are keyed to page number and illustration number. ☐
For medical text—strip across eyes in photographs? ☐

Delivery
DEADLINE for illustrations _____
I will deliver illustrations with manuscript. ☐
I will send illustrations. ☐
By Mail: Certified ☐   Registered ☐
By Messenger ☐
Federal Express ☐   Other ☐
(Name mailing org.) _____
(No. of package) _____

EDITORIAL CHECKLIST (Article or chapter in book)

Check Off: Section Chapter Article Name	Revise/ Comments	Need this Information
MY DEADLINE IS _____	TIP: Shorten your deadline by at least 3 days. This gives you extra time for final checking.	

ORGANIZATION CHECK
   Key Points:
 	
   _____
   _____
   _____
   _____
   _____		

Are my key points clear? Should I shift any section to strengthen or reinforce key points? Is everything in natural time order? Are the dates in order (earliest to latest, or latest to earliest)? Is my description in "space order"? (If you described a place, did you describe it as you want it seen?) Did I develop the ideas from simple or familiar or commonly known to the more complex or unfamiliar? Can I tighten any part?		

CONTENT
   Are my facts accurate?
 	
   Are dates accurate?
 	
   Are personal names accurate?
 	
   Are place names accurate?
 	
   Does the title define the subject and attract attention?
 	
   Are my comparisons clear?		

Are my conclusions clear?		
Are my examples strong?		
Should I divide major points and draw additional contrasts?		
STYLE Do I have a good introduction (lead)?	TIP: Many beginning sentences and paragraphs are written last. Don't worry if you can't start with a socko introduction. Often, you can write it after you develop the entire article or chapter.	
Do I have a strong climactic statement?		
Can I add more active verbs?		
Can I subtract unnecessary adjectives?		
MECHANICS Spelling Check	TIP: Put ms aside for a day or so. Even with a spelling check on a word processor, check for typos.	
Punctuation Check	TIP: Put ms aside before checking punctuation. Check use of periods, commas, semicolons, colons, dashes, hyphens, parentheses, brackets.	
Have I followed special editorial or style capitalization instructions (if any)?		
Have I followed special editorial instructions regarding titles of articles and chapters in books (if any)?		
Have I followed special instructions regarding quotation marks (if any)?		
Have I followed special instructions on page numbers and placement of numbers (if any)?		

BOOK PROGRESS CHECKLIST

Name of book	Special Information or Instructions	Date Completed
CHAPTER BREAKDOWN Number Title		
Number Title		
Number Title		
Number Title		
Number Title		
Number Title		
Number Title		
Number Title		
Number Title		
Number Title		
FRONT MATTER Title Page		
Dedication Page		
Epigraph		
Personal Bio		
Table of Contents		
List of Illustrations (numbered in sequence)		
List of Captions (numbered in sequence)		
List of Tables (numbered in sequence)		
Foreword		
Preface		

Acknowledgments (list people as project is in progress)		
BACK MATTER Notes		
Chapter Notes		
Footnotes	Remarks on style and placement	
End Notes		
Appendices	Style comments: Letter ☐ Number ☐ Classifications?	
Glossary		
Bibliography		
Final Pages Numbered and Checked		
Errors Corrected in Final Copy	Correction: Tape ☐ Liquid ☐ Erasure ☐	
Cover Letter		
Releases		
Final Word Count		

EDITORIAL CORRESPONDENCE CHECKLIST

	Date	Remarks
My letter sent Editor's letter received		
My letter sent Editor's letter received		
My letter sent Editor's letter received		
My letter sent Editor's letter received		
My letter sent Editor's letter received		
My letter sent Editor's letter received		
My letter sent Editor's letter received		
My letter sent Editor's letter received		
My letter sent Editor's letter received		
My letter sent Editor's letter received		
My letter sent Editor's letter received		
My letter sent Editor's letter received		
My letter sent Editor's letter received		
My letter sent Editor's letter received		

RESEARCH
CORRESPONDENCE
LOG

Contact: (Institution or Person)	Date	Nature of Request	Reply

PROPOSAL WORKSHEET FOR THE NONFICTION BOOK

The following worksheet is a valuable guide to writing a nonfiction proposal before one word is put on paper. This checklist will help you organize your thoughts, examine your concepts, and ensure that you say everything you intend to say in your final proposal.

Step One: Thinking It Out

IDEA: State the idea in three sentences. _____
_____
_____
_____
_____

WHY: Why do I want to write this book? _____
_____
_____
_____
_____

WHAT: What is the *purpose* of this book? _____
_____
_____
_____
_____

HOW: How am I qualified to write this book? (relevant experience and education) _____
_____
_____
_____
_____

If I am not yet totally qualified, how will I increase my knowledge and experience? _____
_____
_____
_____
_____
_____

HOW: How will I work on this book? Full time? Part time? _____
_____
_____
_____

WHAT: What are my research resources?* _____
_____
_____
_____

WHERE: Where shall I go for research information?
_____
_____
_____

WHEN: When will I write the book? How long will it take me? _____
_____
_____
_____

WHO: Who is the audience for this book? _____
_____
_____
_____

WHAT: What is the special sales potential of this book? _____
_____
_____
_____
_____

*Reserve your contact lists and private research material at this point. See proposal section.

TELEPHONE EXPENSE LOG

In the course of your work, you will probably make a lot of phone calls. These calls may be to your editor, to your research contacts, or to other sources. It's a good idea to keep track of the calls so that when your bills come in, you'll know what each number on the statement refers to. And, of course, many freelancers are able to take certain tax deductions, including telephone expenses, incurred in the course of their work.

This Telephone Expense Log is an easy-to-use record keeper.

FREELANCE TELEPHONE EXPENSE LOG

Date	Time of Day	Telephone no.	Project	Person Called	Other Contact Numbers	Topic Discussed; Comments

FREQUENT CONTACT SHEET

Publishing House/ Magazine	Address	Telephone no.	Contact	Editor	Direct Telephone no.	Remarks

NONFICTION SUBMISSION LOG: BOOKS

Title of Book	Name of Publisher	Name of Editor	Date Sent	How Sent	Comments	Date Rejected	Date Sold	Rights Sold	Amount

ARTICLE INFORMATION LOGS

The Article Information Log gives you a permanent full-transaction record. You can record the entire process from first query on through submission, acceptance (or rejection), payments (full or kill fees, etc.), receipt of tearsheets, reprint information, photo submissions, and more.

MAGAZINE NONFICTION ARTICLE INFORMATION LOG

Article Sold ☐

Title of Article _____

Query ☐   Date Sent _____
Full MS ☐   Date Sent _____
Cover Letter ☐   Date Sent _____

Editor: _____
Magazine: _____
Address: _____
Phone: _____

Postage Paid _____   How Sent _____

Code Number/Topic _____
Code Number(s) of Photographs _____

Results and Remarks:
   query assigned   ☐   date _____
   rights retained   ☐   remarks _____
   rewrite needed   ☐   remarks _____
   accepted   ☐   date _____
   rejected   ☐   date _____
     remarks: _____
Kill fee ☐ Amount _____ Date Rec'd: _____

Date Published _____
Tearsheets Received ☐   Date _____
Reprint fee _____ Date _____ For: _____
Revised or Condensed Article:
   Fee _____ Date _____ For: _____
   Fee _____ Date _____ For: _____

Photos Sent:
   Black and White   ☐
   Contact Sheets   ☐
   Code Number Sheet ☐
   Rolls   ☐
   Code Number/Topic _____
Code Number(s) of Photographs _____
Photos Returned ☐ Date _____ All ☐ Some ☐
Photos Accepted ☐ Fee for Each _____
   How Many Sold _____
Total Fee _____
Code Number(s) of Photographs Sold _____
Remarks:

Color Transparencies ☐ Size _____
Code Number(s) _____
Transparencies Returned ☐   Date _____
   All ☐ Some ☐
Transparencies Accepted ☐ Fee for Each _____
   How Many Sold _____
Total Fee _____

Remarks:

Title of Article	Name of Publication	Name of Editor	Date Sent	How Sent	Comments	Date Rejected	Date Sold	Rights Sold	Fee

NONFICTION SUBMISSION LOG: MAGAZINES

FICTION SUBMISSION LOG: MAGAZINES

Title of Story	Name of Publication	Name of Editor	Date Sent	How Sent	Comments	Date Rejected	Date Sold	Rights Sold	Fee

THE WRITER'S SPECIAL BILL OF RIGHTS

Since 1978, when the new Copyright Law went into effect, your copyright comes into existence as soon as you create your work. The method of claiming copyright under this newer provision is simple: all you have to do is type: Copyright 1987 (or the actual year in which you create the work). If you send your work to a foreign market, it's not necessary to type out the full word: a lower case c in a circle, or © with the year next to it, are recognized all over the world as copyright symbols.

Copyright gives you the right of ownership to your work and the right to control the distribution and reproduction of the work, as well as any adaptation to any form of media.

In the case of stories, poems, or articles, there's a legal presumption that you're selling the piece just once to the magazine that has agreed to buy it. To be sure, however, that you retain your "Reprint Rights" to resell the piece later, it's best to indicate that you are selling only First North American Serial Rights. (This assumes you're selling to an American or Canadian publication.) Indicate whatever rights you are selling on the upper right-hand corner of your manuscript; type your copyright credit line below that.

To protect your copyright, send your work to copyrighted publications only. (The indicia indicates the copyright symbol and date. This is the material usually printed in very small type and found on the contents or editorial page.) If you send a piece to a non-copyrighted publication without your copyright credit line, you risk having your work assumed into the public domain, where it can be used in any form and at any time without your permission.

It's a good idea never to sell "all rights" to a piece. If you do, you lose your rights to resell the piece or expand it into a book, or to take advantage of the various media available today: TV, screen, stage, radio, video cassettes, recordings—and whatever new technology awaits just around the corner.

Though copyright exists with the creation of a work, writers who believe they may have to take legal action against plagiarism or other infringement want the Copyright Office registration to protect their right to collect damages and attorney fees if they win their cases.

For copyright registration information, write to the Office of Information and Publications, Library of Congress, Washington, DC 20559, Attention: Public Information Specialist, Copyright Office. Or call 202-287-8700. Ask to speak to a Public Information Specialist. You can also leave a recorded message by calling 202-287-9100 and requesting copyright application forms. (Most writers would request Form TX, which covers literary works.) Information requests are free, but a fee must accompany each application for copyright registration. Call for application fee information. Write for other service fees.

You can also write to the Copyright Office and request: Circular R1, "Copyright Basics."

An excellent source of information is a book called *Law and the Writer* by Kirk Polking and Leonard S. Meranus (out of print but available at libraries).

PROTECTING DRAMATIC WORKS

Registering dramatic works (film, TV series, soap operas, plays) with the Writers Guild of America protects both the creator and the potential producer. Indeed, most producers will not look at a submission until the work has been registered with the Guild. In this way, they can avoid accusations of infringing on the material. Writers may be asked to sign a release that registration took place.

Registration also helps the writer who may need support at some time to bolster a claim against misuse of the work.

The Guild will ask the writer to establish the name of the work and the date it was completed before registration (for which a set fee is charged). A copy of the work is deposited with the Guild. Notice (24 hours) is necessary before retrieval. The registration receipt and proper identification must be produced. Occasionally, a court order is required to assure that the work is claimed by the creator or the legal heir or assignee. Registration is renewable after ten years.

The following copyright record log may be helpful
in keeping records of registration:

COPYRIGHT LOG

Name of Copyrighted Material	Date Copyrighted	Rights Assigned to:	Expiration Date	Renewal Date	Writers Guild Registration (if relevant)

INDEX

Dian Dincin Buchman, Ph.D and Seli Groves all too often found themselves, like thousands of other writers, wishing there was a book they could pull from the shelf that would answer all their questions about manuscript preparation and presentation. They finally decided to write it!

Dian Buchman is a former radio commentator and the author or coauthor of twelve books. A past president of the American Society of Journalists and Authors, she originated and chaired the first three national ASJA conferences and also conceived the idea of the Council of Writers Organizations, which represents more than 25,000 writers.

Seli Groves, a past vice-president of ASJA and the CWO, is a longtime newspaper woman, an expert in celebrity interviews, and the life-style feature editor for King Features Syndicate. She is also a contributor to Encyclopaedia Britannica.

Other Books of Interest

General Writing Books

Beginning Writer's Answer Book, edited by Kirk Polking (paper) $12.95
Beyond Style: Mastering the Finer Points of Writing, by Gary Provost $14.95
How to Increase Your Word Power, by the editors of Reader's Digest $19.95
How to Write a Book Proposal, by Michael Larsen $9.95
Pinckert's Practical Grammar, by Robert C. Pinckert $14.95
The 29 Most Common Writing Mistakes & How to Avoid Them, by Judy Delton $9.95
Writer's Market, edited by Glenda Neff $21.95

Nonfiction Writing

Basic Magazine Writing, by Barbara Kevles $16.95
How to Sell Every Magazine Article You Write, by Lisa Collier Cool $14.95
Writing Creative Nonfiction, by Theodore A. Rees Cheney $15.95

Fiction Writing

Creating Short Fiction, by Damon Knight (paper) $8.95
Dare to Be a Great Writer: 329 Keys to Powerful Fiction, by Leonard Bishop $15.95
Fiction Writer's Market, edited by Laurie Henry $19.95
Handbook of Short Story Writing: Vol 1, by Dickson and Smythe (paper) $8.95
Handbook of Short Story Writing: Vol. II, edited by Jean M. Fredette $15.95
How to Write & Sell Your First Novel, by Oscar Collier with Frances Spatz Leighton $15.95
Writing the Modern Mystery, by Barbara Norville $15.95
Writing the Novel: From Plot to Print, by Lawrence Block (paper) $8.95

Special Interest Writing Books

The Children's Picture Book: How to Write It, How to Sell It, by Ellen E.M. Roberts (paper) $15.95
Comedy Writing Secrets, by Melvin Helitzer $16.95
The Complete Book of Scriptwriting, by J. Michael Straczynski (paper) $9.95
Editing Your Newsletter, by Mark Beach (paper) $18.50
How to Sell & Re-Sell Your Writing, by Duane Newcomb $10.95
How to Write Tales of Horror, Fantasy & Science Fiction, edited by J.N. Williamson $15.95
How to Write & Sell a Column, by Raskin & Males $10.95
How to Write & Sell Your Personal Experiences, by Lois Duncan (paper) $9.95
Poet's Market, by Judson Jerome $17.95
Writing Short Stories for Young People, by George Edward Stanley $15.95
Writing Young Adult Novels, by Hadley Irwin & Jeannette Eyerly $14.95

The Writing Business

A Beginner's Guide to Getting Published, edited by Kirk Polking $10.95
How to Write Irresistible Query Letters, by Lisa Collier Cool $10.95
How to Write with a Collaborator, by Hal Bennett with Michael Larsen, $11.95
Literary Agents: How to Get & Work with the Right One for You, by Michael Larsen $9.95
Professional Etiquette for Writers, by William Brohaugh $9.95
Time Management for Writers, by Ted Schwarz $10.95

To order directly from the publisher, include $2.50 postage and handling for 1 book and 50¢ for each additional book. Allow 30 days for delivery.
Writer's Digest Books, 1507 Dana Avenue, Cincinnati, Ohio 45207
Credit card orders call TOLL-FREE
1-800-543-4644 (Outside Ohio)
1-800-551-0884 (Ohio only)
Prices subject to change without notice.

Write to this same address for information on *Writer's Digest* magazine, Writer's Digest Book Club, Writer's Digest School, and Writer's Digest Criticism Service.